POLITICAL KILLINGS
BY GOVERNMENTS

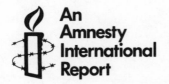

An
Amnesty
International
Report

First published 1983 by Amnesty International Publications
10 Southampton Street, London WC2E 7HF, United Kingdom

Copyright © 1983 Amnesty International Publications

ISBN 0-939994-03-8
AI Index: ACT 03/26/82
Original Language: English

Printed in the United States of America

Index compiled by Steven Pinder

Contents

Introduction

by Theo C. van Boven
former Director of the United Nations Division of Human Rights

Many organizations, groups and individuals concerned with human rights have become more and more aware of the extent and gravity of inhuman practices perpetrated by governments and other forms of organized power in many parts of the world against the life of large numbers of people. These deliberate and brutal killings are carried out in order to liquidate political opponents and other individuals and groups who are suspected of constituting a threat to the vested interests of the established powers.

In my daily work as Director of the United Nations Division of Human Rights these severe and gross violations of the right to life, reported from various regions in the world by reliable sources, including personal testimonies, increasingly became an urgent issue that no one carrying responsibility for the international promotion and protection of human rights could ignore. I felt I had no other choice but to confront the United Nations Commission on Human Rights at the opening of its 38th session on 1 February 1982 with this basic issue of the protection of life and to appeal to the commission to take urgent and effective action. On the global level, the international community is facing a host of intricate human rights problems and different priorities might be established as to how to tackle these problems. I venture to say that, in view of the proportions and severity of extrajudicial executions, absolute priority should be given to strategies and actions to combat these practices.

The awareness that arbitrary deprivation of human life is a most urgent and unavoidable issue for the human rights movement and indeed for the international community as a whole is shared in broad circles. The initiative of Amnesty International, based on its own extensive experience and findings, reflects a *crise de conscience* also prevalent in other human rights organizations and bodies, such as the United Nations Commission on Human Rights and its sub-organs as well as the Inter-American Commission on Human Rights. It may therefore be expected that the international

2

campaign which Amnesty International will be launching on the issue of extrajudicial executions may have a tangible impact inasmuch as this campaign responds to a deep seated conviction of urgency and widely felt sense of human compassion and solidarity. It was for the same reason that earlier campaigns of Amnesty International against torture, against the death penalty and against enforced or involuntary "disappearances" were able, with varying degrees of results, to mobilize many forces within inter-governmental and non-governmental organizations and among the public at large.

The action hitherto developed by the international community against political assassinations shows two major deficiencies. First, it was selective and fragmentary, attention largely being focused on certain situations while other situations deserving equal attention were ignored or remained unknown. A more systematic and comprehensive monitoring of the practice of extrajudicial executions is therefore imperative. The other deficiency is inherent in the *post facto* method of tackling violations of human rights. Consequently, ways and means have to be devised in the preventive sphere, by developing early warning systems and other measures to protect persons who are in immediate danger. Indeed, most of the activities of the United Nations in the field of human rights, and, for that matter, those United Nations activities which report and denounce large-scale, deliberate and arbitrary deprivations of human life are labouring with these problems. Fully aware of the extreme severity of the issue of extrajudicial executions and of its alarming proportions, the UN Commission on Human Rights at its recent session in February–March 1982 made an effort towards a more systematic approach, with the potential of not only remedial and curative action but of preventive action as well. The commission decided to appoint a Special Rapporteur to examine the questions related to summary and arbitrary executions and it requested the rapporteur to submit a comprehensive report to the commission at its next session on the occurrence and extent of the practice of such executions together with his conclusions and recommendations. It would seem that the Special Rapporteur should not limit himself to the in itself very important task of compiling and documenting relevant information on as compre-hensive a scale as possible. The rapporteur should also utilize his potential to address himself, either directly or through the UN Secretary-General, to governments concerned if the urgency of the situation so warrants and such preventive actions may help to save the lives of people in immediate and imminent danger. It is indeed a hopeful and positive coincidence that the decision of the

UN Commission to appoint this Special Rapporteur and the organization of the conference on extrajudicial executions by the Dutch Section of Amnesty International were parallel and mutually supportive actions by important sectors of the inter-governmental and non-governmental human rights community.

In matters of gross and persistent violations of human rights, in situations of extreme human suffering and wherever and whenever survival is at stake, we also have to raise questions of accountability. Who are the perpetrators of these gross violations of human rights, what political authorities carry direct and indirect responsibility and who are their accomplices? Those who hold power must be held accountable for the consequences of its exercise. Mechanisms to enforce accountability must be established. The UN Commission on Human Rights and its Special Rapporteur provide such mechanisms. However, the commission and its rapporteur cannot be the sole instruments for the promotion and protection of human rights and for developing remedial and enforcement action. These UN organs are part of a larger movement whose constituents are the people of the world. Amnesty International forms another segment of that movement and has developed itself into an actor whose moral force carries considerable weight. It is natural that the worldwide campaign on the issue of extrajudicial executions must be motivated by deep felt concern for the victims of these horrible crimes. These crimes must be denounced as crimes against humanity and should be subject to universal jurisdiction. We also have to face the fact that these crimes are not only perpetrated through abstract systems but also, as part of those systems, by persons who are politically accountable and criminally liable for those acts. The establishment and enforcement of accountability is up till now largely and deliberately ignored for the sake of political convenience. This is morally intolerable and indefensible as a matter of principle and of right.

Many people look for solidarity and support in their struggle for justice and survival. They cry out in the wilderness for help. Will their cries continue to fall on deaf ears or is there hope for them as a result of a bolder stand and more courageous action by all those who care?

Theo C. van Boven

Political Killings by Governments

"Did you have permission to kill anyone?
Only suspicious characters. And they gave us orders of the day. And we also had classes—we were students just like the suspects! And we could kill them.

And they gave us special identity cards so that if there were any police around, even if there were more of them than us and we did certain things we could just show them these, so they wouldn't seize us and we could get away. That's what they told us. They gave us cards, so that if we made some great mistake we could kill someone, just like that, and then escape, and the police wouldn't have the power to seize us, we could just show them the cards.

And the police don't do anything?
They don't do anything, nothing. So I realized that the army is a school for murderers. It is as simple as that. They said to me, if you discover your father is in subversive movements—I didn't understand the word—'subversive', they said, is whatever is against the government and is what causes disorder in Guatemala—if your father is involved in groups like that, kill him, because if you don't he'll try and kill us...."

Testimony from a former conscript in the Guatemalan army, February 1980.

"In the beginning only officers' families were killed. At the beginning of 1976, however, the families of common soldiers were also killed. One day at Choeung Prey, I cried for a whole day on seeing women and children killed. I could no longer raise my arms. Comrade Saruoeun said to me: 'Get on with it.' I said: 'How can I? Who can kill women and children?' Three days later I was arrested, in June 1976."

Testimony of a former Khmer Rouge cadre to the International Commission of Jurists.

Hundreds of thousands of people in the past 10 years have been killed by the political authorities in their countries. The killings continue. Day after day Amnesty International receives reports of deliberate political killings by the army and the police, by other regular security forces, by special units created to function outside normal supervision, by "death squads" sanctioned by the authorities, by government assassins.

The killings take place outside any legal or judicial process; the victims are denied any protection from the law. Many are abducted, illegally detained, or tortured before they are killed.

Sometimes the killings are ordered at the highest level of government: in other cases the government deliberately fails to investigate killings or take measures to prevent further deaths.

Governments often try to cover up the fact that they have committed political killings. They deny that the killings have taken place, they attribute them to opposition forces, or they try to pass them off as the result of armed encounters with government forces or of attempts by the victim to escape from custody.

The pattern of killings is often accompanied by the suspension of constitutional rights, intimidation of witnesses and relatives of victims, suppression of evidence and a weakening of the independence of the judiciary.

These killings flout the absolute principle that governments must protect their citizens against arbitrary deprivation of life, which cannot be abandoned under any circumstances, however grave. These political killings are crimes for which governments and their agents are responsible under national and international law. Their accountability is not diminished by opposition groups committing similar abhorrent acts. Nor does the difficulty of proving who is ultimately answerable for a killing lessen the government's responsibility to investigate unlawful killings and take steps to prevent them. It is the duty of governments not to commit or condone political killings, but to take all legislative, executive and judicial measures to ensure that those responsible are brought to justice.

Political killings by governments have certain common features. These are summed up in the definition that Amnesty International uses: "unlawful and deliberate killings of persons by reason of their real or imputed political beliefs or activities, religion, other conscientiously held beliefs, ethnic origin, sex, colour or language, carried out by order of a government or with its complicity". The alternative term "extrajudicial executions" is also used to refer to these killings. They are committed outside the judicial process and in violation of national laws and international standards forbidding the arbitrary deprivation of life. They are unlawful and deliberate: this distinguishes them from accidental killings and from deaths resulting from the use of reasonable force in law enforcement. It also separates them from the category of killings in war not forbidden under the international laws that regulate the conduct of armed conflicts. The fact that they are "extrajudicial" distinguishes them from the judicial death penalty—the execution of a death sentence imposed by a court after a prisoner has been convicted of a crime carrying the death penalty. These extrajudicial executions are political: the victims are selected because of their political beliefs or activities, religion, colour, sex, language or ethnic origin.

* * *

Political killings by governments take place in different parts of the world and in countries of widely differing ideologies. They range from individual assassinations to the wholesale slaughter of mass opposition movements or entire ethnic groups. The scale of the crime is sometimes not known to the international community before it has reached proportions that will damage a whole society for generations to come.

Responsibility

It is often hard to ascertain the facts about political killings by governments. The killers usually wish to conceal or distort the facts, and in some cases so do those reporting the killing. The identity of the victim, how he or she was killed, and by whom, are often uncertain. Eye-witness accounts may be difficult to obtain: sometimes the only witnesses were the killers themselves; sometimes surviving witnesses are themselves at risk. Sometimes the killing itself is hidden and relatives are unable to learn whether the victim is dead or alive. The fact that the victim has been killed may become known, if at all, only months or years later. Even when there is clear evidence of what happened on the spot this may not be enough to prove government complicity.

There are two sides to investigation of reports of politically motivated killings: determining the immediate facts—"what happened"; and assessing whether the government is implicated — "who was responsible".

Discovering what happened includes identifying the victim (if there is a series of killings, compiling a list of victims); finding out about the background of the victim to help establish motives for the killing; gathering information, including medical and forensic evidence, on the cause and circumstances of death; and related medical evidence such as signs of torture or mutilation or marks of handcuffs on the body. Finding out what happened also requires collecting information on the identity of the killers; taking evidence from witnesses; and identifying links between this and other killings.

The assessment of government responsibility poses great problems, even when the actual killers have been clearly identified. Determining responsibility is especially difficult when an established pattern of killings does not exist.

In some cases there is direct evidence of government complicity in a pattern of killings. Examples of such direct evidence include official calls for the elimination of certain categories of political opponent; testimony from defectors from the government who had previously been involved in policy-making or operations; a government practice of labelling killings by government agents as "judicial" executions.

Often, however, the government will deny any responsibility, remain silent or give false explanations. In these cases, assessments have to be made on the basis of circumstantial evidence. Such evidence may include the fact that the victims have been categorized as opponents of the government; evidence that the victims were last seen alive in the custody of government officials or agents; a government record of human rights violations, particularly violent abuses such as torture and "disappearance"; the absence of any reasonable explanation for the killing other than that it was a deliberate government action; a failure by the government to apprehend the killers or to investigate or condemn the killing; contradictions between official accounts of the killing and those from other sources, including such details as inconsistencies in death certificates or autopsy reports, or examples of forged evidence; the government's refusal to cooperate with court decisions in the case. The existence of a consistent pattern of similar killings of government opponents is particulary strong circumstantial evidence when the government makes no convincing effort to identify the culprits and bring them to justice, or otherwise to discourage recurrence of the killings. However, such a pattern does not in itself prove that the government was responsible for a particular killing, nor does identification of the killers as government personnel prove that a killing was the result of a government order or policy.

Political killings by governments have been the subject of investigations by United Nations bodies, by regional intergovernmental bodies such as the Inter-American Commission on

Human Rights, and by international non-governmental organizations such as Amnesty International and the International Commission of Jurists.

Much important investigative work is done by domestic human rights organizations, often under difficult circumstances and at great personal risk to the individuals concerned. A report prepared in 1969 by the Guatemalan Committee of the Relatives of the Disappeared illustrates the investigative methods that can be used. (Tens of thousands of people have been killed in Guatemala since 1966: many were taken into custody and then "disappeared", nothing could be discovered about their fate or whereabouts.) First-hand testimony was provided by eye-witnesses and survivors about the involvement of official security personnel in individual "disappearances" and killings. The equipment and vehicles used in attacks by plain-clothes squads were meticulously identified; efforts were made to establish whether individual items of equipment were government issue and were still in official service. Support provided by regular police and army units during such attacks—cordoning off streets, for example—and their failure to pursue the killers, even when the attacks were carried out in full view of armed security personnel, were documented. Other circumstantial evidence of official involvement included: locations of attacks, in the immediate vicinity of military installations for example; and information used by the attackers such as the home addresses of victims or party or trade union affiliations (information which it was believed could only have come from government sources). Contradictions between official accounts were cited. For example, one government spokesperson denied official involvement in an abduction or killing while other officials justified the same act as a legitimate response to left-wing violence. The government's failure to initiate inquiries into hundreds of the cases brought to official attention and its failure to respond to writs of *habeas corpus* filed on behalf of the "disappeared" were also cited by the committee as indicative of government complicity in "disappearances" and killings.

Within a country there are often serious obstacles to investigation. Sometimes the rule of law has broken down completely. A state of emergency may be in force or the judiciary may not be independent of the executive (or the armed forces in countries under military rule). Sometimes, however, in response to national or international pressure a government sets up an official investigation into reports of political killings with suspected official complicity. Such investigations have produced substantial findings in some cases, but these have not always been taken up.

In Uganda, where at least 100,000 people were killed during the eight-year rule of President Idi Amin, two commissions of inquiry were appointed by President Amin to investigate allegations of human rights abuses by the government. In 1971 a High Court Judge, Mr Justice Jeffrey Jones, was appointed to inquire into the "disappearance" of two United States citizens, Nicholas Stroh and Robert Siedle. In a report released in July 1971 from Kenya, where he had fled in fear of his life, Mr Justice Jones stated his conclusion that the two men had been killed by army officers. The government later implicitly admitted responsibility for the deaths, by paying compensation to the victims' relatives, but no judicial action was taken against those responsible.

In June 1974, after further public concern over "disappearances", President Amin agreed to establish an independent commission of inquiry. The commission consisted of a High Court judge, two police superintendents and an army captain, assisted by a legal counsel and another lawyer as secretary. It worked for six months and produced a report documenting 308 clearly established "disappearances". The report was presented by the Uganda Government to the United Nations Commission on Human Rights in 1975. None of the changes described by the commission of inquiry as necessary to restore the rule of law and prevent abuses by the security forces was implemented. The government continued to attribute most "disappearances" to flight into exile or to killings by guerrillas. In fact the majority of the "disappeared" were killed by the security forces.

Sometimes, after a change of government, human rights violations allegedly committed under the previous government have been investigated, and former officials tried. These investigations and prosecutions have often uncovered important evidence about the circumstances of killings and responsibility for them, although internationally recognized standards for a fair trial have not always been observed in such trials.

In the Central African Empire Jean-Bedel Bokassa, the self-proclaimed Emperor, was deposed in a bloodless coup while absent from the country in September 1979. He was deposed a few months after the killing of between 50 and 100 schoolchildren in Ngaragba prison between 18 and 20 April 1979. These killings, which followed the arbitrary arrest of many schoolchildren and students in Bangui, the capital, caused a storm of international protest and condemnation and led to the creation of a unique five-nation inquiry into the circumstances surrounding the incident.

Amnesty International first publicized the killings on 14 May

1979, reporting that between 50 and 100 deaths had occurred. At first, the government denied that any children under 16 had been arrested or that any of those held had been killed. A week later, however, while attending a Franco-African conference of heads of state in Rwanda, the Emperor admitted to the press that some young people had been killed in April. At the conference five governments — those of the Ivory Coast, Liberia, Rwanda, Senegal and Togo — undertook to send a commission of inquiry to Bangui to investigate the alleged killings.

The commission, the first of its kind in Africa, visited Bangui almost immediately and obtained eye-witness testimonies and other evidence confirming the killings. It interviewed government officials, the prison director, the headmasters of schools in Bangui and schoolchildren who testified to having seen the killings. The commission reported confidentially to the heads of state who had attended the Franco-African summit conference in Rwanda. A month later, on 16 August, the commission's report was made public. By that time several of those who had given evidence to the commission were reported to have been executed or arrested.

Following the September 1979 coup, a commission of inquiry was established by the new government to investigate violations of human rights under Emperor Bokassa. In 1980 six people were sentenced to death after being convicted of having committed murder while Emperor Bokassa was in power; they included former prison guards found guilty of killing children in Ngaragba prison in April 1979, and of killing other prisoners over the previous four years. The six were executed in January 1981. Former Emperor Bokassa was tried in his absence in December 1980; he was accused of responsibility for numerous murders, particularly of political prisoners, and of expropriating and misusing public funds. He was convicted and sentenced to death.*

In Equatorial Guinea President Masie Nguema, whose 10 years in power had been characterized by serious violations of human rights, was overthrown in a military coup in August 1979. The following month the new government decided to create a Special Military Tribunal to try the deposed President and 10 others accused of genocide, mass murder and the systematic violation of human rights. The trial began on 24 September 1979 and lasted for four days. The deposed President repeatedly justified all his past actions on the grounds that he was head of state and refused to acknowledge the jurisdiction of the court. Substantial evidence was presented to indicate that President Masie Nguema had been responsible for the deaths of hundreds of prisoners and had

*Amnesty International opposes the use of the death penalty in all cases.

intervened directly to cause some killings. Some of the other defendants, who included a former vice-president and several prison guards, were also charged with complicity in murder. The court passed the death sentence on the former President and six others and sentenced the four other defendants to periods of imprisonment. No right of appeal was allowed. The seven men condemned to death, including President Masie Nguema, were executed by firing-squad less than five hours after they had been sentenced.

Official Cover-up

The facts about political killings by governments are often hidden or distorted by those responsible. The official cover-up can take many forms: concealing the fact of the killing, for example, by making prisoners "disappear"; blaming killings on opposition forces or independent armed groups; or passing off unlawful killings of defenceless individuals as the result of armed encounters or escape attempts.

One means of covering up political killings by governments is to conceal the identity of the perpetrators, claiming that the killings were the work of clandestine groups over whom the government has no control.

The following testimony by a Salvadorian refugee was given to an Amnesty International mission which visited refugee camps in Honduras in August 1981:

> "Thirty heavily armed men wearing army combat vests, but masked with hoods lettered 'death squad' came to my village and seized and killed a number of *campesinos* [peasants].
> They went then to the neighbouring village of Santa Helena, seized Romilia Hernández, aged 21, raped and then decapitated her. Her relatives buried her head: the rest of her body was burned by her murderers. The head had been left in front of her relatives' house. The members of the 'death squad' were evacuated that day by a Salvadorian army helicopter."

Thousands of people are believed to have been victims of political killings by the government in El Salvador since the military coup of October 1979. Among the agencies cited have been regular military forces, special security forces including the National Guard, the National Police and the Treasury Police, and a nominally civilian paramilitary unit called ORDEN (now renamed *Frente Democrático Nacionalista,* Democratic Nationalist Front), established in 1967 to carry out a clandestine "counter-terror" campaign against government opponents. The authorities have claimed that ORDEN's operations ended with its official disbandment in October 1979 and that any atrocities perpetrated by paramilitary groups in the countryside are carried out by independent extremist groups or "death squads" out of its control. But there are reports indicating that the unit remains in existence and that the so-called "death squads" are in fact members of ORDEN or other off-duty or plain-clothes security personnel acting in close conjunction with regular military and security units.

In the Philippines the authorities have commonly responded to allegations of human rights violations by claiming that they are the result of armed conflict, particularly with the New People's Army, the armed wing of the Communist Party of the Philippines. People reported to have "disappeared" are described as having "gone underground". Those killed by military personnel are said to have been killed in combat.

An Amnesty International delegation visited the Philippines in November 1981. It was presented with details of a number of cases in which the authorities asserted that the victims had been killed in encounters with members of the New People's Army. Such was the explanation given by Captain Montano, commander of the 431st Philippine Constabulary (PC) Company, for the killing of two men in Catalunan Grande, Davao. At a commission set up to investigate the killings witnesses testified that the two victims had been taken from their homes by soldiers of the PC and that one of them had been severely beaten in front of his family. The autopsy reports showed that the victims had sustained several gunshot and stab wounds and that one of them had been strangled. The commission's findings gave no support to Captain Montano's allegation that the victims had died in an encounter.

In India in December 1980 the Minister of State for Home Affairs stated in a written reply in the lower house of the Indian parliament that 216 "Naxalites" (members of the Communist Party of India [Marxist-Leninist]) had been shot dead by police in Andhra Pradesh state since 1968. He added that the shootings were "a sequel to armed attacks launched by Naxalites on police". Eye-witness accounts obtained by Amnesty International and other investigating bodies indicate that a number of the victims had been arrested and, in some cases, tortured before being shot.

Creating a cover-up can involve fabrication of evidence. For example, in Colombia there have been a number of unexplained killings by official forces in rural "militarized" zones, where the army has for some years had violent clashes with guerrillas. On the morning of 26 April 1981 an army patrol entered the ranch of Ramón Cardona in Albania, Caquetá, dragged the ranch owner and two others from the house and took them into the nearby hills. Screams were heard. The next day the three men were found dead, their bodies bearing the signs of severe torture. According to reports of the incident, neighbours were ordered to transfer the bodies to a clearing, where soldiers placed a small quantity of food, an empty army knapsack and a camouflage shirt by the bodies. The soldiers then told local people and army officers who arrived to view the bodies that the supplies were evidence that the men had been guerrillas. An army press bulletin subsequently declared that the men had ambushed an army patrol and been killed in an exchange of fire.

In Argentina, Ana Lia Delfina Magliaro was taken from her home in La Plata on 19 May 1976 during an anti-subversive operation. For 50 days her family was unable to obtain any information about her whereabouts, despite numerous inquiries. On 2 August they learned that she was being held in a federal police station in Buenos Aires. The family visited her twice but on the third day, 4 August, they were told that she had been transferred by the military police of the First Army Corps to the city of Mar del Plata. On 20 September the family filed a petition for *habeas corpus*.

Two days later they were notified by the local police that Señorita Magliaro had been "killed in combat" in Mar del Plata. A photograph was produced showing the dead girl, gun in hand, in an unspecified place. According to her death certificate she had been killed on 2 September.

On 9 October 1976, Señorita Magliaro's mother received the following official response to the petition for *habeas corpus*: "This person was received into custody at the 34th Federal Police Station on 9 July 1976 at 12.00 after being detained by the army. She was transferred by the military police of First Army Corps to Mar del Plata on 4 August 1976."

At no time had the girl's family been told that she had been released. Her sudden and violent death, in a town more than 400 kilometres from her home, when she was known to be in the custody of the army, makes the official account of her death, that she had been "killed in combat", extremely improbable.

Sometimes political killings by governments are announced by the authorities as executions. In Ethiopia it was announced on 24 November 1974 that 60 prominent political prisoners had been executed the previous night by firing-squad. They included the

14

head of state Brigadier General Aman Andom, relatives of the
deposed Emperor Haile Selassie, and senior officials and military
officers of the former Imperial government. The former head of
state had in fact been killed in a gun battle with an opposing
faction of the military government, and the 59 political detainees
were shot without trial.

'Disappearances'

Many political killings by governments have been concealed
because the victims have "disappeared": the authorities have tried
to hide both the fact of the killing and their own responsibility.
The victims of this technique of political repression are taken into
custody and then "disappear": their friends and relatives cannot
find out where they are held or what has happened to them.
Sometimes the victims of "disappearance" are later discovered in
prison, or released; sometimes it is learned that they have been
killed.*

"Disappearances" and political killings by governments are
frequently connected. Often victims of extrajudicial execution are
secretly abducted before being killed: the "disappearance" dis-
guises the killing. But a "disappearance" is not always followed by
death, nor are all killings preceded by "disappearance".

It was in Guatemala in the mid-1960s that a group of relatives of
"disappeared" people used the term by which this human rights
violation is now known throughout the world. They called themselves the Committee of the Relatives of the Disappeared. In
Guatemala many victims of "disappearances" have been killed;
only extremely rarely has a "disappeared" person later been found
in custody or reappeared alive. It has, however, often been
difficult to verify the fact that an individual who has "disappeared"
has died. Bodies have been recovered from secret graveyards in a
state of decomposition that makes it impossible to ascertain their
identities. Corpses have been found at roadsides far from where
abductions took place, so badly mutilated that identification was
difficult or impossible. The practice of leaving bodies in public
places appears to be intended to terrorize potential opposition, as
does the open reporting in the Guatemalan press of assassinations
and the finding of bodies.

*Amnesty International considers that a "disappearance" has occurred whenever
there are reasonable grounds to believe that a person has been taken into custody
by the authorities or with their connivance and the authorities deny that the victim
is in custody.

In Argentina, following the March 1976 military coup, thousands of suspected "subversives" were abducted by the police and security forces and taken to secret camps under military control. At least 6,000 people are known to have "disappeared" since the military coup; their fate remains unclear. Evidence has gradually emerged of "disappeared" prisoners being tortured and killed, their bodies being disposed of secretly. The precise number killed remains unknown. While the majority of "disappearances" took place during the period from 1976 to 1978, since the beginning of 1979 Amnesty International has received information on over 100 politically motivated abductions followed by "disappearance". In some cases the "disappearance" was temporary and the individuals concerned were later released or recognized as official detainees; the bodies of other victims were subsequently found; some of the victims remain "disappeared" and there is no news of their whereabouts.

In Guinea President Sekou Touré's government has failed to account for approximately 2,900 prisoners who "disappeared" after being arrested for political reasons between 1969 and 1976. Many are believed to have died as a result of torture, execution, deliberate starvation or inhuman prison conditions.

In Afghanistan thousands of people "disappeared" after the People's Democratic Party (PDP) government came to power following a military coup in April 1978. The precise number of "disappearances" and killings is not known. The first details about "disappearances" in Afghanistan date from the period several months after the April 1978 coup when imprisoned officials and others associated with the former government "disappeared". Accounts were received from former prisoners that political detainees were brought to Kabul from all over Afghanistan. Some died of torture during interrogation, while others were taken immediately after interrogation to places of execution in the Ministry of the Interior and at the AGSA (Internal Secret Security Police) headquarters. Still others went initially to Kabul's main prison—Pule Charchi—a few miles outside the city, and are still missing.

According to former prisoners, groups of detainees were removed from Pule Charchi prison, particularly in late 1978 and early 1979, and are believed to have been shot in "Polygoon" valley near the prison. One group included 130 political prisoners (many of them students) who had already been imprisoned under the previous regime because of their orthodox Islamic views. Eyewitness accounts say they resisted transfer from prison for execution. The army was called in, and on the night of 30 May

1979, 117 of them were killed between 4.30 and 11.30 am.

On 9 October 1979, shortly after President Nur Mohammed Taraki was overthrown by Mr (later President) Amin, 50 political prisoners, including prominent citizens and opposition leaders, are reported to have been taken away at night from Pule Charchi prison, never to be seen again. There is only one account of the "disappearance" of a prisoner in daylight. When former Prime Minister and Ambassador to Pakistan Nur Mohammed Etemadi was told he would be released from prison he was asked to collect his personal belongings and say goodbye to his friends. An official car came for him on the afternoon of 22 August 1979, and he has not been seen since. It is widely believed that he was killed.

On 27 December 1979 the new government of President Babrak Karmal took power, ousting President Amin. On 28 December President Karmal declared a general amnesty, as a result of which the government said 12,000 political prisoners had been released (although independent sources considered the true figure to be lower). During its mission to Kabul in February 1980 Amnesty International met relatives of some of the thousands of prisoners who were known to have been arrested but had not been released under the general amnesty. In the absence of any other information, relatives hoped that these prisoners might still be alive in provincial prisons or other prisons outside Afghanistan. The Karmal government, however, has said that all those not released in December 1979 had been killed before it came to power. Government officials told Amnesty International that they had a list of 4,584 people who had been killed, but that they believed the number of killings and "disappearances" was actually higher.

The killings

Political killings by governments have been committed in most, if not all, the regions of the world. The cases in this report show that they are not confined to any one political system or ideology. Further examples are given here of political killings since 1980 believed to have been carried out by official forces or others linked to the government. The circumstances of the killings and the nature of government involvement vary from country to country. Some governments have been shown to be responsible by their wilful failure to investigate adequately or to prevent further killings.

The victims — individuals and entire families — have come from all walks of life and from many political persuasions and religious faiths. Politicians, government officials, judges, lawyers, military officers, trade unionists, journalists, teachers, students and school-children, religious workers and peasants: all have lost their lives. In some cases well-known political figures have been publicly assassinated; in others whole villages have been wiped out, and the news has not reached the outside world for weeks or months. Often the victims belonged to the political opposition—often they were simply members of a particular ethnic group or lived in an area targeted for security operations.

In El Salvador, thousands of people have been killed by the security forces since the military coup of October 1979. The victims have included not only people suspected of opposition to the authorities, but thousands of unarmed peasant farmers living in areas targeted for military operations in the government's counter-guerrilla campaign. People monitoring government abuses such as journalists, church activists, comunity workers, political militants and trade unionists have been intimidated, arrested and killed. Patients have even been abducted from hospital beds by security forces and killed.

On 3 January 1982 Archbishop Arturo Rivera y Damas of San Salvador stated that he estimated that 11,723 non-combatants had been killed in El Salvador during 1981. In July 1981 the Centre of Information and Documentation of the University of Central America in San Salvador estimated that some 6,000 civilians had been killed in the first six months of the year. In the same month another Roman Catholic source put the death toll in the previous 18 months at 22,000.

Testimonies received daily by Amnesty International implicate all branches of the Salvadorian security services in the killings. In addition to the regular armed forces El Salvador also relies on special security forces such as the National Guard, which combines police and military functions, the National Police and the Treasury Police. All these units have repeatedly been named in reports of political killings. So has a nominally civilian paramilitary unit called ORDEN (now renamed *Frente Democrático Nacionalista*, Democratic Nationalist Front), established in 1967 to carry out a clandestine "counter-terror" campaign against government opponents. Recently the Atlactl Brigade, a special new unit trained by US military advisers, has been blamed repeatedly for killings of unarmed peasants in rural areas.

The Salvadorian authorities continue to maintain that any abuses were perpetrated by security or armed forces personnel exceeding their authority. They have also on several occasions stated that officers or troops implicated in these abuses have been removed from duty, or assigned to non-combatant positions.

The authorities have also claimed that atrocities in rural areas were perpetrated by independent extremist groups or "death squads" out of government control. Other reports, however, have indicated that the so-called "death squads" are made up of members of ORDEN or other off-duty or plain-clothes security personnel acting in cooperation with the regular armed forces.

In Libya the Third Congress of the Libyan Revolutionary Committees issued a declaration in February 1980 calling for the "physical liquidation" of enemies of the 1969 revolution living abroad. Since then at least 14 Libyan citizens have been killed or wounded in assassination attempts outside Libya.

In Uganda, the widespread unlawful killings of the eight-year military government of President Idi Amin ended only with the overthrow of the regime in 1979. In the aftermath of the armed conflict, a high level of criminal violence continued, with many unexplained but possibly politically motivated murders. Opponents and supporters of the government and members of the security forces were killed under the successive governments of Yusuf Lule, Godfrey Binaisa, and the Military Commission. Former President Milton Obote returned to power after elections in 1980. Instability continued, and early 1981 saw a series of guerrilla attacks. Many civilians — particularly alleged political opponents — were arrested by the army and there were reports of torture and killings in military custody. Unarmed civilians are also reported to have been killed by security forces operating against guerrillas in the countryside.

In Iran, in addition to the large number of officially announced executions which have taken place since the revolution of February 1979 (more than 4,500 at the end of November 1982), Amnesty International has received many reports of executions which have not been announced and may not have been preceded by a trial. In other cases it is clear from the circumstances of the killings that no legal proceedings took place. Because of the difficulty of obtaining reliable and detailed information from all parts of Iran, it is often not possible to know whether a death is the result of a judicial decision or could be described as an extrajudicial execution. Sometimes prisoners who have previously been sentenced to a term of imprisonment have been executed, but it is not known whether this is the result of an arbitrary decision, or whether new legal proceedings have taken place.

Some months after the revolution, fighting broke out between government forces and members of the Turkoman ethnic group. Four Turkoman leaders were arrested and imprisoned in Evin

Prison, Tehran, from where they were kidnapped, taken away and killed. The then President of Iran, Abolhassan Bani-Sadr, sent two missions to discover how the Turkoman leaders had died and the findings of both missions were that they had been kidnapped and killed by the Revolutionary Guards.

Members of the Baha'i religion have been killed in circumstances suggesting official involvement. Amnesty International knows of no case in which anyone has been prosecuted in Iran in connection with such a killing. On 12 January 1981 Professor Manuchihr Hakim was shot dead by unknown assailants in his office. He was a physician and professor at the University of Tehran and had been a member of the supreme governing body of the Baha'is of Iran for many years. Three days before his assassination Professor Hakim had been visited by two Revolutionary Guards and interrogated at length about his activities as a Baha'i. Before this interrogation Professor Hakim had received threats to his life.

Kurds have also been killed in circumstances which suggest strongly that extrajudicial executions have taken place. One report described the killing of 18 workers on 14 September 1981 at a brick-laying factory near the village of Saroughamish. According to the report Revolutionary Guards arrested the workers, put them against a wall and machine-gunned them.

A report received in October 1982 referred to the killing by Revolutionary Guards of 51 people in the village of Dehgaz in the Caspian region between June and September 1981. The reason for these killings was reported to be the villagers' alleged sympathy with the opposition People's Mujahadeen Organization of Iran (PMOI).

In Colombia members of the political opposition have been killed by the security forces, and peasant farmers summarily executed by the army in rural areas where counter-insurgency operations are carried out.

Extensive isolated regions of the country have been "militarized" to combat guerrilla groups operating there, and other special security measures imposed to control the local population. Freedom of movement in these areas is strictly controlled, and supplies of food, clothing and medical goods limited to deprive guerrilla forces of material support. Controls have been enforced through the threat of arbitrary detention, interrogation and torture at local army posts or temporary bivouacs, and death. People have been detained on suspicion of aiding guerrillas and then killed by army units. Others have been killed after routinely reporting to a local army post to have their safe-conduct passes

20

stamped as required.

On 20 June 1982, the state of siege that had been in force in Colombia for most of the past 34 years was lifted. However, reports of killings of peasants by army counter-guerrilla units in rural areas, particularly Central Colombia, have continued since 20 June 1982.

In Chad there have been reports of killings of civilians and soldiers no longer in combat by forces loyal to Hissène Habré (who was sworn in as President on 21 October 1982) after they occupied the capital, N'Djamena, in June 1982 and moved on to consolidate Habré's control of the country. Eye-witness accounts have described defeated soldiers of the opposing *Forces armées tchadiennes*, Chadian armed forces, and some of their civilian collaborators, being killed by the pro-Habré forces, the *Forces armées du nord*, armed forces of the north. For example, Karhyom Ningayo, the mayor of Moundou, was shot in front of his family by soldiers of the *Forces armées du nord* while he was trying to escape from the town in early September 1982.

In Namibia, where South African military forces are in conflict with nationalist guerrillas of the South West Africa People's Organisation (SWAPO), church leaders and others have reported that civilians have been killed by South African soldiers because they were thought to support or sympathize with SWAPO.

In Bolivia, following the July 1980 military coup, Amnesty International received reports that security forces were involved in numerous "disappearances" and political killings. In the mining areas of Huanuni, Catavi and Siglo Veinte, where strikes against the coup had been organized, troops attacked with tanks and heavy weapons to put down any resistance to the military take-over. The armed forces also took over or destroyed the miners' radio stations. On 21 August 1980 Amnesty International publicized reports that in early August troops had killed a group of miners and peasants in the mining district of Caracoles, in the department of Oruro, that women had been threatened and ill-treated by troops, and the bodies of the dead removed before they could be identified. A large number of people were reported missing.

In Chile, during the first few months after the 1973 military coup thousands of people were reported to have been summarily executed; between 1973 and 1979 hundreds — mainly political activists, trade unionists and peasants — "disappeared" after being arrested by the security forces of the army, navy, air force and *carabineros* (uniformed police), all coordinated by the *Dirección de Inteligencia Nacional* (DINA), National Intelligence Directorate. The "disappearances" and killings which took place between 1973 and 1979 remain officially unexplained. In August 1977 the DINA was dissolved and replaced by the *Central Nacional de Informaciones* (CNI) — Chilean secret police.

Since 1977, a number of alleged members of banned political parties and organizations, such as the *Movimiento de Izquierda Revolucionaria* (MIR), Movement of the Revolutionary Left, have died in the custody of the CNI, in circumstances which indicate that they may have died after torture, or may have been deliberately killed by other methods. A number of other killings have been described officially as the result of "confrontations" with members of the security forces, such as the CNI. Some victims were reportedly abducted by members of the security forces before being killed.

People are reported to have been killed also by the *Comando de Vengadores de Los Mártires* (COVEMA), Command for the Vengeance of Martyrs, one of several secret organizations believed to consist of members of the security forces and to be connected with the CNI.

In some instances of alleged "confrontations" and deaths in custody, official investigations have been started, but reports indicate that once the CNI or other security forces have been implicated the investigation has been passed from the civilian courts to the military courts. Military courts have consistently failed to bring those responsible to justice.

In Mexico there have been reports of a number of killings in which regular army units have been involved or some other official link is known or suspected. On 25 July 1982, for example, a military detachment entered Coacoyult in the municipality of Ajuchitlán, Guerrero, and took 13 peasants away with them. Of the 13, five were later found dead.

In East Timor, which has been occupied by Indonesia since December 1975, there have been numerous reports of people being executed after surrendering to, or being captured by, Indonesian armed forces. In September 1981 as many as 500 people, among them non-combatant women and children, were alleged to have been killed after capture by Indonesian forces in Lacluta in the district of Viqueque. An Indonesian official has stated publicly that between 60 and 70 people were killed in the incident including women and children. He asserted that the victims died in armed combat after refusing repeated calls to surrender. Amnesty International is not at present able to assess the conflicting accounts of what happened at Lacluta.

In the Republic of Korea (South Korea) at least 40 people were killed when army paratroopers dispersed a peaceful student demonstration in Kwangju on 18 May 1980. Amnesty International has received reports and eye-witness acccounts alleging that paratroopers clubbed people on the head indiscriminately and bayonetted them; that many of the dead were shot in the face, and that others were stabbed to death. Reportedly, at least 1,200 civilians died in disturbances in the following nine days; the South Korean authorities said that 144 civilians, 22 soldiers and four police officers died. Amnesty International has also received allegations that eight people arrested in connection with disturbances in Kwangju were beaten to death on 16 July 1980 by Special Forces troops and their bodies buried in the prison grounds.

In Syria since 1980 there have been several reported incidents of killings by the security forces. On 27 July 1980 hundreds of prisoners — most of them believed to have been members of the outlawed Muslim Brotherhood — were reported to have been killed in Palmyra (Tadmur) desert prison by the *Saray al-Difa'*, Special Defence Units, a special military force under the command of President Assad's brother, Rifa'at Assad. On the night of 23 April 1981 Syrian security forces reportedly sealed off parts of the town of Hama, carried out house-to-house searches, dragged people from their homes, lined them up in the streets and shot them. Amnesty International received the names of over 100 of those reported killed.

On 2 February 1982 violent clashes between security forces and Muslim Brotherhood fighters, following the discovery of a hidden cache of arms, developed into a near-insurrection in the town of Hama. The town was encircled by Syrian troops and security forces and subsequently bombarded from the air and the ground. A news blackout was imposed by the authorities. In early March, after the fighting had ended, reports of massacres and atrocities began to reach the outside world. Most reports indicated that at the start of the fighting government officials and their families in Hama were systematically sought out and killed by the rebels. Later, however, massacres were reported to have been committed by government forces partly through aerial bombardment but also by troops on the ground as they regained control of the town. Unofficial estimates put the killings by security forces at over 10,000, but Amnesty International was not able to make its own assessment of the number killed.

Syrian security forces have also allegedly been responsible for the assassination abroad since 1980 of several prominent opponents of the Assad government.

In the aftermath of the Israeli invasion into the Lebanon, hundreds of Palestinian and Lebanese civilians in the refugee camps of Chatila and Sabra in West Beirut were massacred between 16 and 18 September 1982. The Israeli armed forces were in military control of the area at the time; an Israeli judicial commission was later established to determine whether the Israeli authorities had any responsibility for the killings. Headed by the chief justice of the Israeli Supreme Court, the commission met in open and closed sessions and took evidence from military officers and high-ranking officials. The Lebanese President Amin Gemayel also initiated an inquiry, whose proceedings have been secret. As of November 1982 the inquiries were still in progress. Amnesty International had called on the United Nations to establish an impartial and international inquiry, and had called on the Lebanese and Israeli authorities to cooperate with such an investigation.

In Iraq several political suspects in custody were allegedly poisoned in 1980 shortly before they were released. Two of the cases involved Iraqis who were examined by doctors in the United Kingdom after they left Iraq. Both were found to be suffering from thallium poisoning. Thallium is a heavy metal used commercially in rat poison. One of the two died; the other was said to have recovered.

Well over 20 Yugoslav political emigres have been assassinated since the early 1970s, including two in 1980, and emigre circles have frequently alleged that Yugoslav state security service (SDS) agents were responsible. The findings of courts outside Yugoslavia have in several cases supported such allegations.

Mass liquidation

Several governments in the past two decades have decided on the wholesale liquidation of political opposition. The death toll in these purges has run into the tens and hundreds of thousands, sometimes in a matter of months.

In Indonesia, following an abortive coup attempt in September 1965, the army leadership under Generals Suharto and Nasution consolidated its control over the government and called for the destruction of the communist party (PKI), which they blamed for the coup attempt. General Nasution was reported to have told an army staff conference that "all of their [PKI] followers and sympathizers should be eliminated" and to have called for the party's extinction "down to its very roots". The first killings in nearly every province were initiated by the army. In some areas the army was assisted by gangs of youths belonging to *Ansor*, an affiliate of the *Nahdatul Ulama* a fundamentalist Muslim party. PKI members were loaded into lorries and driven away to be killed and buried in mass graves. Other bodies were dumped in rivers, or victims were towed out to sea and their boats sunk. Alleged members and supporters of the PKI and its affiliated organizations were killed, along with their families and thousands of Chinese. It is estimated that at least 500,000 people were killed in Indonesia in the nine months between October 1965 and June 1966. This figure was given by Admiral Sudomo, the head of the government security agency.

In Kampuchea under *Khmer Rouge* rule (1975–1979) at least 300,000 people were killed in a series of purges directed at "counter-revolutionaries" and other "undesirable elements". Nearly all high-ranking officers of the former Lon Nol government, senior officials, police officers, customs officials and members of the military police appear to have been executed during the days immediately after the *Khmers Rouges* came to power. Subsequent purges were directed at lower officials of the former Lon Nol government; at intellectuals, teachers and students, often described by the *Khmers Rouges* as "the worthless ones"; at members of ethnic minorities, especially the Cham, a Muslim people; at currents within the ruling movement who were out of line with the leadership; and at alleged "counter-revolutionaries".

In Uganda at least 100,000 and possibly as many as half a million people were killed by the security forces during the eight years of President Idi Amin's rule (1971–1979). The victims included members of particular ethnic groups, religious leaders, judges, lawyers, students, intellectuals and foreign nationals.

In Ethiopia thousands of people were unlawfully and deliberately killed by the security forces after the Provisional Military Government assumed power in 1974 — particularly during the government's "Red Terror" campaign of 1977 and 1978. In February 1977 the government publicly ordered the security forces, including armed civilian officials, to "apply red terror and revolutionary justice" to the members and supporters of the opposition Ethiopian People's Revolutionary Party, which it accused of being "counter-revolutionary" and spreading "white terror". At the peak of the "red terror", from November 1977 until about February 1978, an estimated 5,000 political opponents of the government were killed in Addis Ababa alone.

In Burundi at least 80,000 people are believed to have been killed in just two months — May and June 1972. There had been a power struggle between the dominant Tutsi ethnic group and the numerically larger Hutu for some years, and a Hutu-inspired rebellion began on 29 April 1972 in the capital, Bujumbura, and in several provinces. Two provincial capitals were overrun in the course of the uprising and some 2,000 people killed, including a brother-in-law of the president and a provincial governor.

On 30 April a government counter-attack began. Martial law was declared and a curfew imposed. The army, assisted by the *Jeunesse révolutionnaire Rwagasore*, Revolutionary Rwagasore Youth, the paramilitary youth movement of the ruling party, began killing anyone believed to be connected with the uprising, as well as any other Hutu leaders or potential Hutu leaders. In the capital and in the provinces Hutu were loaded into jeeps and lorries, clubbed to death and buried in mass graves. There were also a number of killings arising from personal disputes, and a number of Tutsi were killed as well.

According to a British reporter, David Martin, who visited Burundi during this period:

"...at Bujumbura bulldozer tracks could clearly be seen from the air near the main airport where victims had been buried in mass graves and open trenches were waiting for more bodies. To be educated — albeit only to primary level — or to have a job, was a death sentence for a Hutu. Diplomats were hiding their cooks and gardeners at their official residences. The banks in the capital said they had lost over 100 Hutu employees from clerks upwards, all of whom were believed to be dead. At the cable office, where before the uprising and repression twenty-five Hutu had worked, only two were left. One large Belgian company said that every single Hutu employee had disappeared and almost all of them were thought to be dead. One of the few surviving Hutu employees I spoke to in Bujumbura said that he had tried to escape but had been stopped at a road block, beaten up and told to go back. He had not been involved in the uprising so could not understand why they should do anything to him. He knew many of his friends who had also not been involved but had been killed. Subsequently I learned he too had disappeared."

* * *

This report is published as part of a campaign that will mobilize all Amnesty International groups around the world in a concerted effort to halt political killings by governments.

Amnesty International is a worldwide movement that works for the release of prisoners of conscience, fair and prompt trials for political prisoners, and an end to torture and the death penalty. It is unconditionally opposed to the judicial or extrajudicial execution of any prisoner. It acts against political killings of non-prisoners "when it is reasonable to believe that they are part of a consistent pattern or can otherwise reasonably be assumed to be the result of a government policy to eliminate specific individuals, or groupings, or categories of individuals, by instant execution rather than arrest and imprisonment". Amnesty International holds as a matter of principle that the torture and execution of prisoners by anyone, including opposition groups, can never be accepted. Governments have the responsibility of dealing with such abuses, acting in conformity with international standards for the protection of human rights.

Amnesty International has tried to combat extrajudicial executions for a number of years. It has appealed to governments, has publicized the killings internationally, and submitted information to expert United Nations (UN) bodies and other intergovernmental organizations. In April 1979 Amnesty International appealed to the UN Secretary-General to convene an emergency meeting of the UN Security Council to halt an upsurge of executions and political killings throughout the world.

In early 1982 the Dutch Section of Amnesty International organized an International Conference on Extrajudicial Executions. Some 120 participants from 30 countries, including independent experts, members of intergovernmental and non-governmental organizations, members of the Amnesty International staff and sections, and activists from other human rights groups came together to explore possibilities for stepping up activities against these killings.

This report includes edited papers prepared for that conference. A report on the conference, together with the conclusions and recommendations reached by members of its working parties, is given at the end.

Because the facts about extrajudicial executions are so often concealed and because of the time needed to conduct a thorough investigation, it may be several years before a clear picture emerges. Sometimes important pieces of evidence emerge only after the practice has stopped — after a change of government or other political changes. For these reasons the approach taken in this book is largely historical. Each country case study covers a situation where a clear pattern of killings has emerged. Most of the papers describe killings which have occurred since 1970.

Political killings by governments have been committed in more countries than those considered in this book: it is in no sense exhaustive.

Amnesty International wishes to express its thanks to the many individuals who participated in the seminar and the conference and whose ideas are reflected in this report.

Guatemala : political killings by government

"The soldiers came; we went to the mountains; there we found tree trunks and stones where we hid. A group of soldiers came from behind, they came in behind us. They seized three of us; they took them to the mountains; they tied them up in the mountains and killed them with machetes and knives. There they died. Then they asked me which ones were the guerrillas, and I didn't tell them, so they slashed me with the machete; they raped me; they threw me on the ground and slashed my head with the machete, my breasts, my entire hand. When dawn came, I tried to get home. By then I could hardly walk. I came across a girl from our village and she was carrying some water. She gave me some and took me to her house.

"The army also seized my 13-year-old brother Ramos and dragged him away and shot him in the foot and left him thrown on the ground. My brother and my parents and my other brothers and sisters had been in the house. The soldiers said 'They are guerrillas, and they must be killed.' My brother saw how they killed my parents, my mother, my brothers and sisters and my little one-year-old brother; the soldiers machine-gunned them to death when they arrived in the village. Only my brother, Ramos, and I are alive. Our friends are giving us injections and medicines. We can't go to the hospital at Cobán. I think they would kill us there."

Testimony from a 17-year-old Kekchi Indian woman, from the hamlet of Chirrenquiché, Cobán, Alta Verapaz, Guatemala. The attack took place on 7 April 1982.

Tens of thousands of Guatemalans have been killed under successive governments since 1966. They have been killed, for political reasons, by regular military and police units, both on and off duty, in uniform and in plain clothes; by official security guards assigned to government functionaries; by private security guards often led by former police or military personnel; and by "death squads".

This term refers to armed groups, often made up of off-duty military and security personnel, which have had a major role in the killings. Amnesty International believes that these groups are linked to the government.

The victims have come from all sectors of Guatemalan society: peasants and Indians, trade unionists, church activists, political leaders, journalists and members of the legal profession. Many individual victims have been assassinated because they were prominent in groups suspected of opposition to the government; or in groups that the government feared might provide a focus for opposition. Others have been killed because they belonged to such organizations, or have been shot during public activities such as non-violent demonstrations. Peasants have been massacred in areas where guerrillas were believed to be active, apparently to prevent the guerrillas gaining supplies and support, and to intimidate the population. Other people have "disappeared" after being taken into custody: their fate remains unknown.

President Méndez Montenegro (1966 to 1970)

The rise in the use of killing as a means of political repression has generally been associated with the fierce counter-insurgency campaign carried out under civilian President Julio César Méndez Montenegro. The campaign developed in response to the activities of several armed guerrilla movements which originated in the early 1960s. Police units which assisted in the counter-insurgency campaign – the *Policía Militar Ambulante*, Mobile Military Police, and the *Policía de Hacienda*, treasury or border police – have been repeatedly named in subsequent years as having carried out killings in the countryside. In the capital, Guatemala City, various units of the National Police, including the semi-autonomous intelligence branch known until recently as the *Policía Judicial*, judicial police, have been frequently cited in reports of "disappearances" and killings. Special legislation commissioned large landowners and their administrators as law enforcement officers authorized to bear arms; they were thus incorporated in the counter-insurgency campaign and were reportedly responsible for killings. Armed squads organized by the *Movimiento de Liberación Nacional*, National Liberation Movement, an extreme right-wing political party, have also been cited as responsible for killings.

The presidency of Méndez Montenegro also saw the emergence of urban "death squads" which in the following years carried out thousands of killings in Guatemalan cities. In the month before his inauguration, leaflets were distributed announcing the formation of the *Mano Blanca*, "White Hand", which pledged itself to "eradicate national renegades as traitors to the country". Soon killings of real or suspected opponents of the government began; often the victims received threats by telephone or leaflet before their murder. Sometimes the assassins left behind leaflets claiming responsibility. In other cases the initials of groups claiming responsibility were scrawled on walls or slashed in the victims' bodies. The *Mano Blanca* led the way, but 20 more such groups announced their formation in the first year of the Méndez Montenegro presidency.

The Minister of Foreign Affairs, Alberto Fuentes Mohr, drew the President's attention to persistent reports that government security forces and high-ranking officers were behind killings and other illegal acts. (In 1979 Alberto Fuentes Mohr was assassinated in broad daylight in Guatemala City.)

Evidence of government responsibility for these human rights violations included direct testimony by eye-witnesses and survivors that official security personnel had been involved. Support provided by regular police and army units during "death squad" attacks, such as cordoning off streets, combined with their failure to pursue attackers, even when the assaults had been carried out in full view of armed security personnel, suggested at least the tacit complicity of the regular police and security forces. The government also failed to initiate genuine inquiries into the hundreds of cases brought to official notice, or to respond to numerous writs of *habeas corpus* filed on behalf of the "disappeared".

However, the government repeatedly maintained that the "death squads" were out of its control, and succeeding governments have adhered to this explanation.

President Arana (1970 to 1974)

By the end of the Méndez Montenegro presidency, the authorities acknowledged that the military threat posed by the guerrilla movements had been crushed. Colonel Carlos Arana Osorio, who succeeded Méndez Montenegro as President, had led the counter-insurgency campaign. During his presidency the "death squads" continued to operate, turning their attention to non-violent opponents and suspected potential opponents of the government. President Arana had come to office promising to put an end to "subversion", and in November 1970 he declared a state of siege. A new wave of repression began. In June 1971, for example, the *New York Times* reported that at least 2,000 Guatemalans had been assassinated in the six months following the imposition of the state of siege. Violence increased towards the end of this presidency.

President Laugerud (1974 to 1978)

President Arana was followed in office by General Kjell Laugerud. The state of siege was lifted and during the first two years of the Laugerud presidency the level of violence subsided, although it did not cease. In 1975 Amnesty International presented to the Guatemalan Government and the Organization of American States a list of 134 people who had "disappeared" or been killed in the seven-month period between 1 July 1974 and 31 January 1975. The list was necessarily incomplete, as it recorded only instances reported in the press. It appears that during this period killings abated when opposition to the government was at a low level, but upsurges of political activity or social unrest were met by an increase in violence.

After a severe earthquake in February 1976 the government moved against various opposition groups on the pretext that it was maintaining law and order and that summary executions were necessary to protect lives and property. One target was the centre-left political grouping, the *Frente Unido de la Revolución* (FUR), United Front of the Revolution, which had gained control of the Municipality of Guatemala City, and was pressing to obtain unoccupied lands for the capital's slum dwellers. The Director of Administrative Services of the Municipality, Rolando Andrade Peña, was gunned down in the centre of the city some two weeks after the earthquake. In March, the political grouping's leader, Manuel Colom Argueta, who as mayor of Guatemala City during the Arana presidency had served as a focal point for opposition to the President's policies, was himself wounded in an armed attack. He published an open letter to the President, marshalling the evidence that led him to conclude that the *Policía Regional*, regional police, had been responsible for the attack on his life. (On 23 March 1979 Colom Argueta was machine-gunned to death in broad daylight in Guatemala City.)

President Romeo Lucas García (1978 to 1982)

In the months before the 1978 elections Guatemalans enjoyed an increase in political freedoms. For the first time in many years public demonstrations were permitted. But when General Romeo Lucas García became President a new wave of violent repression was unleashed. Leaders of the effort to reform the trade union movement were assassinated; peaceful demonstrators were killed by security units. A new "death squad", the *Ejército Secreto Anti-Comunista*, Secret Anti-Communist Army, issued to the press on 18 October 1978 a list of people they claimed to have "tried and sentenced to death". The list included trade unionists, student leaders, journalists, academics and lawyers. Two days later Oliverio Castañeda, president of the students' association of the University of San Carlos, became the first person on the list to die. He was murdered by heavily armed assailants using five cars. He was attacked on a busy street corner in Guatemala City in full view of large groups of armed security officers who were there to control an annual demonstration in commemoration of the 1944 Revolution. No action was taken to apprehend the killers.

In December 1978, Pedro Quevedo y Quevedo, secretary general of the trade union organizing at the Coca Cola bottling plant, was murdered. His successor, Israel Marquez, escaped three attempts on his life before taking refuge in the Venezuelan Embassy in 1979. Manuel López Balan replaced Israel Marquez but was knifed to death in Guatemala City on 5 April as he did his rounds in his Coca Cola delivery van. In May 1980 union activist Marlon Mendizabal was murdered as he waited for a bus outside the plant. In June 1980, almost the entire leadership of the *Central Nacional de Trabajadores* (CNT), the trade union congress, which included several leaders at the Coca Cola bottling plant, were abducted as they met to discuss funeral plans for a Coca Cola union leader murdered some days before. Eye-witnesses recognized some of those who carried out the abduction as members of the official security forces. Vehicles used in the abduction were official issue models. The abduction took place within one block of the National Palace; the street was closed to traffic by uniformed National Police officers, while an estimated 60 plainclothes officers entered the CNT headquarters. The cars of some of those abducted were later recovered from a National Police garage. Conflicting versions of events were given by different government officials. Various officials denied that the trade unionists had ever been arrested but Vice-President Francisco Villagran Kramer publicly announced that he had filed a writ of *habeas corpus* on behalf of the detainees with the proper judicial authorities. Later, Minister of Labour Carlos Alarcón Monsanto informed Amnesty International groups that those detained had subsequently been released. None has ever been seen again. There have since been unconfirmed reports that some of the missing people's bodies have been found among the many corpses uncovered in secret cemeteries throughout the country.

In February 1981 Amnesty International issued a report stating that since President Lucas García took office in July 1978, the organization had learned of the seizure without warrant, and subsequent killing, of some 5,000 Guatemalans. Contrary to claims by successive governments that the death squads were not under official control, the report concluded that there was no evidence of pro-government, clandestine groups operating independent of government control. Citing testimony from recent defectors and from the survivor of a "disappearance" the organization stated that the links between the death squads and the authorities had been particularly blatant during the presidency of Lucas García, and that officials at the highest level had been involved in orchestrating a centralized program of illegal actions.

The Guatemalan Government rejected the findings of the report and accused Amnesty International of interfering in its internal affairs. It failed to comment on any of the individual cases cited in the report.

The "disappearances" and killings continued throughout 1981. Records kept by Amnesty International, which are inevitably incomplete, list a minimum of 2,011 people killed between 1 January and 30 June 1981. In the period from 1 July to 31 December 1981 Amnesty International recorded a minimum of 2,569 killed. Victims included lawyers, journalists and religious activists. During 1981 Amnesty International noted an increase in the number of medical staff killed, and several mass killings of Indian peasants. These killings appeared to be linked to an increase in rural insurgence: they were apparently intended to eliminate potential bases of support for guerrillas and to intimidate medical staff into refusing assistance to the wounded.

President Efraín Ríos Montt

In June 1982 General Efraín Ríos Montt assumed the presidency following a military coup which took place in March 1982. The *junta* which took power after the coup stated that it intended to ensure a return to respect for human rights. A number of positive steps were taken: some civilian officials who had been involved in repression under the previous government were arrested, and the judicial police was disbanded. Immediately after the coup killings by death squads in urban areas appeared to have decreased. But in succeeding weeks, new special police units were formed to carry out the functions previously performed by the judicial police, and persistent reports were received of massacres by the regular armed forces and newly formed civilian militias of peasants in rural areas.

In a special briefing issued in July 1982 Amnesty International said:

"There have been consistent reports of massive extrajudicial executions in Guatemala since General Efraín Ríos Montt took power in March 1982. Following a pattern not significantly different from that implemented under previous governments, Guatemalan security services continue to attempt to control opposition, both violent and non-violent, through widespread killings including the extrajudicial execution of large numbers of rural non-combatants, including entire families, as well as persons suspected of sympathy with violent or non-violent opposition groups. Information available to Amnesty International, including press reports, testimonies of witnesses and official government pronouncements, repeatedly identifies the regular army and civilian army auxiliaries organized as 'civil defence' units under the Ríos Montt government."

International concern about human rights violations in Guatemala has often been expressed. Guatemala has appeared again and again in the reports of human rights watchdog organizations, and on the agendas of international and regional bodies. In March 1981 the Commission on Human Rights of the United Nations requested the UN Secretary-General to establish direct contact with the Government of Guatemala on the human rights situation and to collect information from all relevant sources. Evidence of the UN's continuing concern about the human rights situation in Guatemala was the appointment in 1982 of a special rapporteur on Guatemala to make a thorough study of the situation.

In September 1982 the Inter-American Commission on Human Rights of the Organization of American States visited Guatemala; it had first requested an on-site observation in 1973. In 1981 the commission had presented a well-documented report which concluded that an alarming climate of violence had prevailed in Guatemala in recent years, either instigated or tolerated by the government which had proved itself unwilling or unable to contain it.

Mass killings in Indonesia (1965 to 1966) and Kampuchea (1975 to 1979)

"In 1975 ... we were made to change policy: the victory of the revolution had been too quick. If the population was not wiped out immediately, the revolution would be in danger because the republican forces, the forces of Sihanouk, the capitalist forces would unite against it. It was therefore necessary to eliminate all these forces and to spare only those of the Communist Party of Kampuchea. It was necessary to eliminate not only the officers but also the common soldiers as well as their wives and children. This was also based on revolutionary experience. In the past, Sihanouk had killed revolutionaries, but their wives, children and relatives had united against him and had joined us. That must not be repeated against us now. In the beginning, however, only officers' families were killed. At the beginning of 1976, however, the families of common soldiers were also killed. One day at Choeung Prey, I cried for a whole day on seeing women and children killed. I could no longer raise my arms. Comrade Saruoeun said to me: 'Get on with it.' I said: 'How can I? Who can kill women and children?' Three days later I was arrested, in June 1976."

Testimony of a former Khmer Rouge *cadre to the International Commission of Jurists.*

The government-instigated killings in Indonesia in 1965 and 1966 and in Kampuchea in 1975 to 1979 rank among the most massive violations of human rights since the Second World War. A conservative estimate of the number of people killed in Indonesia is 500,000. In Kampuchea the number of victims was at least 300,000.

Both in Indonesia in 1965 and 1966 and Kampuchea in 1975 to 1979 the governments decided to transform the political map within their countries through the physical liquidation of the political opposition. Elements of such a policy may exist elsewhere, for example in the killing of political leaders or selected members of political groups. The scale of the Indonesian and Kampuchean tragedies resulted from the governments concerned being intent on the permanent physical eradication of all opposition in the case of Kampuchea, and of left-wing opposition in the case of Indonesia.

In Indonesia the principal targets were members of the Indonesian Communist Party and its affiliated organizations–the trade unions, the women's organization (*GERWANI*) and the peasants' association (*Barisan Tani Indonesia*). Their families were killed too. In Kampuchea, the victims came from several categories including personnel of the former government, members of the bourgeoisie and intelligentsia and from currents *within* the revolutionary movement that were out of line with the leadership. In addition, many members of ethnic minorities were killed in both countries.

In both Indonesia and Kampuchea the killings were not committed in a period of armed conflict. Resistance was minimal in both cases.

Indonesia (1965 to 1966)

At the beginning of 1965 the Indonesian Communist Party (PKI) was the largest political party in the country. It operated legally and had declared its commitment to peaceful social change.

On 30 September 1965 a group of nationalist army officers led by Lieutenant-Colonel Untung attempted to stage a coup against the government of President Sukarno. Six army generals were killed. The coup attempt was crushed by General Suharto in 24 hours.

During the next few weeks the army leadership under Generals Suharto and Nasution consolidated their control over the government. At the same time they linked the leadership of the PKI with the coup attempt and blamed the PKI for the killing of the six generals. As a result of these accusations PKI members were attacked by mobs and several thousand members were arrested in Jakarta. But it was in Central Java, a long-time PKI stronghold, that the killings of PKI members began.

The arrival in Central Java of two battalions of the Indonesian "Red Berets", or Army Paracommandos (RPKAD), signalled an army decision to crush the PKI in Central Java before annihilating the party throughout the country. The RPKAD began killing PKI members in Central Java in mid-October 1965, when the PKI was already in disarray and was not offering armed resistance. An

Indonesian Government White Paper later argued that the RPKAD had arrived in Central Java to prevent a large-scale insurgence, but there is little evidence that there was in fact a threat of insurrection.

There was no set pattern to the killings that then began and that claimed the lives of an estimated 500,000 Indonesians in the following nine months. However, certain features recurred. Everywhere local officials of the PKI and its affiliated organizations were rounded up and shot. In many cases whole families were killed; it was often said by the perpetrators that the liquidation of entire families would serve to eliminate the communist menace for all time.

The first killings in nearly every province were initiated by the army. In some areas the army was assisted by gangs of youths belonging to *Ansor*, an affiliate of the *Nahdatul Ulama*, a fundamentalist Muslim party. In Java, Bali and Sumatra, night after night for months, local army commanders loaded lorries with captured PKI members–their names checked off against hastily prepared lists–and drove them to isolated spots nearby for execution, usually by bullet or knife. In some cases the bodies were grotesquely mutilated before being buried in hurriedly dug mass graves.

In the town of Kediri in Central Java, a PKI stronghold, some 7,000 PKI supporters are estimated to have been killed. In Banjuwangi in East Java, 4,000 people were killed in a few days. In East Java most people were executed with long sugar-cane knives and sickles; the slaughter often assumed a ritualistic and ceremonial character. In several places the killers held feasts with their bound victims present. After the meal each guest was invited to decapitate a prisoner–apparently to involve as many as possible in the killings.

As the purge accelerated in November 1965 headless bodies covered with red flags were floated down rivers aboard rafts and heads placed upon bridges. Every day for several months riverside residents in Surabaya in East Java had to disentangle bodies that were caught on jetties. At one point so many bodies from Kediri filled the Brantas river that the downstream town of Jombang lodged a formal protest complaining that plague might break out. In the small mill town of Batu so many were executed within the narrow confines of a small police courtyard that it was decided that it would be simpler to cover the piles of bodies with layers of cement rather than bury the victims.

The killings in Bali began sporadically in the west of the island during November 1965. The arrival of RPKAD troops on the island soon ensured that the killings assumed a systematic character. Armed with machine-guns, commandos scoured villages in groups of 25, in some cases executing the entire male population. Hundreds of houses belonging to known communists, their relatives and friends were burned down within a week of the purge being launched. The occupants were slaughtered as they ran out of their dwellings.

A commonly accepted estimate of deaths resulting from the operation in Bali is 50,000, with women and children among the victims. All Chinese retail shops in Denpasar and Singaradja were destroyed and their owners executed after summary judgments were issued convicting them of financing the PKI. The killings of Chinese on Bali were soon followed by persecution elsewhere in Indonesia, claiming thousands of Chinese lives and leading to the exodus of many other Chinese from the country.

By early 1966 the killings had reached virtually all of Indonesia. From Java to Bali they had spread to Sumatra, Kalimantan (Borneo), Sulawesi, Lombok, Flores and Timor. In one incident alone in the city of Medan, North Sumatra, some 10,500 prisoners were reportedly killed in the space of a few days. On the island of Belitung, birthplace of D.N. Aidit, the PKI chairman, hundreds of victims were thrown down disused mineshafts and others towed out to open sea where their boats were sunk.

The responsibility for the killings in Indonesia rested unquestionably with the Indonesian Army which by then effectively controlled the government. Before the killings General Nasution had called for the extirpation of the PKI, and he was reported to have told an army staff conference as the RPKAD arrived in Central Java that "all of their [PKI] followers and sympathizers should be eliminated". During a visit to Surabaya he called for the PKI's extinction "down to its very roots". In mid-November, as the killings gathered momentum, General Suharto signed an order authorizing an "absolutely essential clearing out" of the PKI and its sympathizers from the government. This directive, No. 22/KOTI/1965, set up "special teams" to carry out the order and authorized the teams to request military assistance "if necessary".

During the first few months of the killings, President Sukarno and some of his ministers tried to bring them to a halt, but without success. On 11 March 1966 President Sukarno's government was formally replaced by the military government of General Suharto, still in power in 1982.

The precise number of people killed will probably never be known. An inquiry team set up by President Sukarno at the end of 1965 estimated that there had been 87,000 deaths. However, this figure referred only to the island of Java, and the inquiry took place at a time when the killings were just starting in many other places. In late 1966 an investigation commissioned by the army and conducted by the University of Indonesia estimated that one million people had perished since the start of the killings. There are some indications that this estimate may be too high. Admiral Sudomo, the head of the chief government security agency (KOPKAMTIB), later scaled the figure down to 500,000. In addition, some 750,000 people were arrested and detained without charge or trial. Several hundred were still in detention in 1982. In a period of less than a year all the leading figures of the PKI, Indonesia's largest political party, together with countless thousands of its members and supporters, had been killed.

Kampuchea (1975 to 1979)

On 17 April 1975 forces of the revolutionary communist movement known as the *Khmer Rouge* entered the capital of Cambodia, Phnom Penh, overthrowing the government of Lon Nol. This was the outcome of several years' civil war between the *Khmer Rouge* and the Lon Nol government, which was supported by the United States of America. Upon taking power the new government immediately set out to evacuate all cities and towns and to execute the leadership of the former government.

By 1975 the population of Phnom Penh had swollen to more than two million, roughly one third of the total population, as a result of the civil war and the US bombing and destruction of agriculture. On the morning of 17 April 1975 *Khmer Rouge* troops toured the city ordering the population to evacuate the city within three days on pain of death. In practice many residents were given less than an hour in which to leave. Those who refused, procrastinated or showed some opposition were beaten or shot dead. Old people, disabled, children, pregnant women and hospital patients were all forced to leave the city without distinction.

During the evacuation many people are known to have died. Some were killed by *Khmer Rouge* troops in order to keep the marchers moving or to maintain discipline. Refugees from Phnom Penh have spoken of people, particularly the young, dying on the roadside. One of the city's leading physicians, Dr Vann Hay, said that on his march from Phnom Penh he saw the body of a child about every 200 metres.

In the following days other cities and towns were evacuated including Battambang (200,000 inhabitants), Svay Rieng (130,000), Kompong Chhnang (60,000), Kompong Speu (60,000) and Siem Reap (50,000). The loss of life from this gigantic shift of population is incalculable.

The population of the evacuated cities and towns, known as the "new people" as distinct from the "base people" (the peasantry), were moved to agricultural sites where they were forced to work long hours on irrigation works and the cultivation of rice under strict discipline. Slight infringements of discipline were frequently punished by execution.

The evacuation of Cambodia's cities was accompanied by the first of several purges — that of the officer corps and senior officials of the former Lon Nol government. Nearly all high-ranking officers, senior officials, police officers, customs officials and members of the military police appear to have been executed during the days immediately after 17 April 1975. Detailed and independent accounts have been obtained from the towns of Phnom Penh, Battambang, Siem Reap, Pailin and Kompong Speu. In some places all officers from lieutenant upwards were executed. Even this distinction of rank was often lost, and in the first few months after the revolution some local authorities were apparently given a free hand in deciding whom to execute. On the forced marches from Phnom Penh *Khmer Rouge* forces were permitted to pull out of the marching columns anyone they suspected of being associated with the former administration and kill them on the spot.

Many accounts of these killings are now available. For example:

> "The chairman of Tuk Phok district, named Miec Vay, summoned 50 guerrillas from various villages of his district and gave them this oral order: 'The former Lon Nol soldiers are our enemies. We must kill all enemies to celebrate the day of victory. This is the order of our leader Pol Pot. Anyone who refuses to kill is disobeying orders and must inflict on himself due punishment.' We obeyed the district chairman's order and the 50 of us killed 2,005 Lon Nol soldiers." (From evidence before a revolutionary tribunal in Phnom Penh in August 1979.)

It appears from such testimonies that the killings were not simply an act of revenge conducted in the heat of victory but were carried out in fulfilment of a central government policy.

Non-commissioned officers, army privates, minor officials and village headmen were treated differently from region to region. Some were executed in the days following the *Khmer Rouge* victory, others were sent to hard labour camps while others were allowed to return home. In late 1975, however, the policy towards lesser officials changed; systematic executions of this group then began and continued into 1976.

The killings of former Lon Nol officers and officials extended to their families. Wives and children were executed to prevent them becoming opponents of the new government.

The killings of former government personnel were soon followed by executions of .members of the bourgeoisie and intelligentsia. The rationale behind this practice was reflected in a document issued by the Executive Bureau of the Eastern Region Party Committee:

> "We must heighten our revolutionary vigilance as regards
> those elements who have served in the administrative
> machinery of the former regime, such as technicians,
> professors, doctors, engineers and other technical personnel.
> The policy of our Party is not to employ them in any
> capacity. If we run after this technology, we will feel that
> they submit to us and we will use them, but this will create
> the opportunity for enemies to infiltrate our ranks more
> deeply with every passing year and this will be a dangerous
> process."

In line with this policy intellectuals–often crudely identified as those who wore spectacles–were singled out for particularly harsh treatment and in many regions of the country were summarily executed. Many refugees report that from early 1976 intellectuals, teachers and students, often described by the *Khmer Rouge* as "the worthless ones", disappeared from their places of work and were presumed to have been killed. A former *Khmer Rouge* cadre recalled that in Kompong Cham province it was decided "to arrest 'the worthless ones', in other words, intellectuals, teachers, pupils beyond the seventh grade. The country had to be rid of them. That was the decision of the Central Committee, just as it had been its decision to wipe out the soldiers in 1975–1976."

Besides the killing of political and social groups designated enemies of the revolution, many thousands of individuals were executed on such grounds as minor infringements of work discipline. Offences such as illicit sexual relationships, criticizing or challenging official instructions, resistance to the introduction of communal eating (after 1977), and even laziness were often punished by death.

From 1975 to 1977 there were regional variations in the pattern of repression. In the Eastern Zone, although former Lon Nol officers had been killed in 1975, conditions do not seem to have been as harsh as elsewhere. This resulted from political differences between regional authorities and the central government in Phnom Penh.

These differences came to a head in 1978 when the central government leadership under Pol Pot launched what was, in effect, an invasion of the Eastern Zone (which bordered on Viet Nam). The long-simmering conflict between the centre and the more moderate eastern communists exploded into open warfare in May 1978, and the following months saw one of the most massive purges of the entire *Khmer Rouge* period. Tens of thousands of people including officers and soldiers, together with their fathers, mothers, wives and children were executed. The victims included all Eastern Zone cadres who could be traced, people evacuated from the cities in 1975, and anyone with Vietnamese relatives and connections. It has been estimated that 100,000 people were killed in this purge because the party centre in Phnom Penh had decided that the Eastern Zone was led by "Khmer bodies with Vietnamese minds". A former rubber plantation worker, one of many refugees interviewed, said:

> "They killed all the Eastern Zone cadres, and ordinary
> people who committed the most minor offences, such as
> talking about one's family problems at night. Every day they
> would take away three to five families for execution. We
> would hear them screaming for help...". (Kiernan, *Khmer
> Bodies with Vietnamese Minds: Kampuchea's Eastern Zone,
> 1975–1978*, Monash University, 1980.)

The local party leader So Phim and almost the entire Zone Committee, the local military hierarchy and all but two members of the regional committees were executed. Executions of cadres are reported to have occurred in almost all districts, sub-districts and villages. A number of villages, including So Phim's home village, are reported to have been entirely wiped out.

Members of ethnic minorities also were the victims of repeated massacres with thousands of Chinese, Vietnamese, Lao and Thai being killed. The Cham, a Muslim people, were singled out for especially harsh treatment. From the early days of the Democratic Kampuchean Government (*Khmer Rouge*) all religious activity was rigorously repressed and religious leaders executed. In the case of the Cham this was followed in early 1976 by a ban on the use of their native language, the suppression of their religious beliefs and forcing them to raise pigs and eat pork. Cham villages were dispersed and the Cham people told that they were a weak link in the nation. Cadres are reported to have told Cham leaders in 1977 in the south-west region: "... the Chams are hopeless. They abandoned their country to others. They just shouldered their fishing nets and walked off, letting the Vietnamese take over this country."

Executions of Cham leaders and dignitaries and the populations of entire villages soon followed. In Stung Trang, lorries loaded with Chams were reportedly pushed down steep ravines. The district of Kompong Xiem, in the province of Kompong Cham, with five hamlets and a total population of 20,000, was reported to have been razed to the ground and all its inhabitants killed. In the district of Koong Neas, in the same province, out of an estimated 20,000 inhabitants there were reportedly only four survivors. It is now conservatively estimated that more than half of the total 1975 Cham population of 400,000 was killed between 1975 and 1978.

Of all the mass killings carried out during the *Khmer Rouge* rule of Kampuchea, the most clearly documented are those that took place at Tuol Sleng, also known as S21. Tuol Sleng was a former school in Phnom Penh used by the *Khmer Rouge* as a centre for torture and execution. Careful records were kept of prisoners and the prison archives, which have survived virtually intact, show that nearly 15,000 people were liquidated there. Some of the victims of Tuol Sleng were *Khmer Rouge* soldiers from the Eastern Zone; others were members of the government or other Kampuchean communists suspected of opposing the government.

At any one time the prison held an average of 1,000 to 1,500 prisoners. Most were held for a short time, tortured and forced into writing confessions before being killed. The names of alleged co-conspirators elicited through confessions were recorded and elaborate charts drawn up showing lines of "contacts" in coloured inks.

The rate of executions increased after October 1977. On 15 October 1977 the prison record books show 418 killed; on 18 October, 179 were killed; on 20 October, 88 and on 23 October, 148. The highest single figure was 582 recorded executions on 27 May 1978. In many cases, as with the veteran communist Hu Nim, the cause of death was recorded as "crushed to bits".

In January 1979 the Government of Democratic Kampuchea was overthrown by the forces of the Kampuchean United Front for National Salvation, after an invasion by Vietnamese troops in December 1978. The country was renamed the People's Republic of Kampuchea. The new government established a special tribunal which in August 1979 tried *in absentia* Pol Pot and Ieng Sary, the

Prime Minister and Foreign Minister in the Democratic Kampuchea Government. They were charged with genocide and both were sentenced to death. During the trial, witnesses testified to having participated in torture and killings committed on the orders of the authorities. Victims of imprisonment and torture also testified against the accused *Khmer Rouge* leaders. Documents on prisons and mass graves were presented to the court.

In August 1981 Democratic Kampuchea's Foreign Minister Ieng Sary, attending a United Nations conference on Kampuchea in New York, was confronted with some of the evidence of killings during a press interview. Ieng Sary admitted that the documents were genuine and confirmed the killing of Hu Nim and the existence of Tuol Sleng. He also acknowledged what no other *Khmer Rouge* leader had admitted before–that it was official policy to liquidate people accused of opposing the regime. He justified the policy by saying that "the circumstance was proletarian dictatorship. We were in the middle of class struggle."

Despite the magnitude of the killings in Indonesia and Kampuchea, the international community did little to try to stop them. The United Nations first took official note of the human rights situation in Kampuchea in March 1978 when there was considerable discussion at the UN Human Rights Commission. It asked the Sub-Commission on Prevention of Discrimination and Protection of Minorities to consider the matter in 1979. Several governments and non-governmental organizations submitted information and the sub-commission decided to investigate further. The Government of Kampuchea responded by calling it "impudent interferences in internal affairs". In January 1979 the commission received a report about human rights violations in Kampuchea, but by that time the *Khmer Rouge* government had been overthrown.

To some extent this inaction may have been caused by lack of information at an early date. The killings in Indonesia and Kampuchea took place in conditions of considerable secrecy and in some cases it was weeks and even months before any details became available outside the country. When information did emerge, there were accusations that it was exaggerated for political reasons. Prompt research by impartial external investigative bodies, using such techniques as interviews with refugees, might have led to earlier and more effective measures to counteract the killings.

In Indonesia the killings subsided only when the principal target, the communist party, had been destroyed. In Kampuchea they ended only when the government was overthrown.

Uganda under President Amin (1971 to 1979)

"... I was held down with soldiers treading on my wrists and legs, and pins were stuck under my toenails.... The next day we were ordered to crawl over some very sharp stones which cut our knees and hands till they bled. The two in front were ordered to go outside. I heard two shots and then four of us were ordered to go outside too. I thought this was the end but we were just told to load the dead bodies into a Landrover."
Testimony of a prisoner held in the Naguru Public Safety Unit barracks, Uganda, during the government of President Idi Amin.

At least 100,000 and possibly as many as half a million people were killed by the security forces during the eight years of President Idi Amin's rule in Uganda. Systematic and deliberate killings by government forces began in the first month of President Amin's military government and the practice was rapidly institutionalized as a means of eliminating opponents and potential opponents.

Those who were not killed outright, or shortly after arrest, were mostly tortured by the army, the intelligence service or a special police unit, and then killed. Few political detainees survived long. The victims included members of particular ethnic groups, religious leaders, judges, lawyers, students and intellectuals, and foreign nationals. The impunity with which the security forces were permitted to kill political opponents and criminal suspects created the conditions in which many other people were killed by members of the security forces for criminal motives or even arbitrarily.

From Uganda's independence from Great Britain in 1962 until 1971, Uganda was ruled by a civilian government led by Prime Minister, then President, Milton Obote. In January 1971, President Obote was overthrown by his army commander, General (later Field Marshall and Life-President) Idi Amin Dada. Parliament was abolished, political parties were suspended and constitutional safeguards against the misuse of power were removed. The police force was greatly weakened and the independence of the judiciary undermined by constant interference by the security forces.

The security forces were strengthened and their powers expanded. The armed forces were given wide powers of arrest over civilians. Two new security institutions were established. The Public Safety Unit, a special police unit, was set up in 1971 and given powers to "shoot to kill", ostensibly to suppress armed robbery. The Bureau of State Research was established under the direct control of the President as the powerful state intelligence agency replacing President Obote's General Service Unit. The headquarters of these two agencies at Naguru (near the capital, Kampala) and Nakasero (Kampala) respectively, along with the military police barracks at Makindye (Kampala), became notorious for torture and killing.

A number of decrees signed by President Amin facilitated the killing of civilians by government forces. In 1971 the security forces were given wide powers of arrest without warrant, and the power to detain indefinitely without charge any person suspected of subversion. Under Decree Number 7 of May 1972, any security official was empowered to "use any force he may deem necessary" to arrest or prevent the escape of anyone suspected of armed robbery. This decree legitimized a policy of "shooting to kill" which was frequently used to justify killings by security officers, whether in uniform or plainclothed. Under Decree Number 8 of May 1972, the security forces were given immunity from prosecution—retroactive to the 1971 coup.

The possibility of obtaining a fair trial, undermined by a 1973 decree empowering military tribunals to judge certain cases previously in the jurisdiction of the civilian courts, was further reduced by the killings of judges, lawyers and defendants. On 21 September 1972, Chief Justice Benedicto Kiwanuka was dragged from Court Chambers, taken away in an army vehicle and killed–apparently in retaliation for his demands for the independence of the judiciary and his attempts to uphold the right to *habeas corpus*. In 1973, a businessman, Samson Ddungu, was shot dead in the street after a trial in which he had been acquitted against the wishes of a senior Public Safety Unit officer. His lawyer, Enos Ssebunya, was arrested at the same time and severely tortured.

Political killings by government agents in Uganda were generally carried out in secrecy — particularly after unfavourable international publicity about certain killings in public — as it became understood by the government that a practice of causing suspected opponents simply to "disappear" enabled a semblance of normality to be maintained in the country. From 1971 onwards many people were arrested by the security forces and made to "disappear" with the authorities denying any knowledge of them. Those arrested were often bundled into the back or trunk of a security forces vehicle and taken to a military barracks, the Bureau of State Research, the Public Safety Unit, or to a secret "safehouse" under State Research control. Prisoners were arrested and detained without legal formalities or judicial processes, held incommunicado and often without official records. Nearly all prisoners were severely tortured; most either died under torture or were killed in other ways. Prisoners were sometimes ordered at gunpoint to kill other prisoners. In this method of execution prisoners were lined up: one was given a hammer and ordered to beat another prisoner to death with it; he in turn was then killed by another prisoner, and so on, with the last survivor of the group being shot by a prison guard. Prisoners' bodies were frequently dumped in rivers or forests. Occasionally, the bodies (usually mutilated) were returned to relatives by security officers on payment of large bribes.

A minority of people arrested on political grounds were held in police custody and transferred to Luzira Upper Prison, a maximum security prison under the civil jurisdiction of the Ugandan Prisons Service, where ill-treatment was less frequently alleged.

On 15 February 1977 the 18 Anglican bishops of Uganda issued a public statement deploring "disappearances" and killings–attributing them to "the activities of some members of the security forces". On the following day the bishops were summoned to meet President Amin. Three prisoners–who had evidently been tortured–were made to read out so-called confessions. These stated that they had conspired with Archbishop Luwum, former President Obote, President Nyerere of Tanzania, members of former President Obote's ethnic group (the Langi) and the adjoining Acholi to overthrow President Amin with Chinese weapons.

Later that day Archbishop Luwum was taken from the other bishops by soldiers. Two cabinet ministers, Mr Charles Oboth-Ofumbi and Lieutenant Colonel Wilson Oryema, were also arrested. The following day the government announced that the three men had died in a car accident while trying to overpower the driver in an attempt to escape. Information which later became widely known indicates that the three men were, in fact, killed by security officers and the car accident faked.

During the next three months thousands of Acholi and Langi were arrested and killed in many parts of Uganda. Soldiers visited government offices, the university, hospitals and other institutions with lists of people to be arrested. According to some reports, a "death list" had been prepared in advance on a countrywide basis. It comprised all Langi and Acholi prominent in the professions, educational institutions and government service. Among the victims of the killings were students, teachers, civil servants, businessmen, soldiers and police officers. In the north of the country, where the Langi and Acholi come from, whole villages were massacred.

In September 1977, 12 people accused of treason and of plotting with Archbishop Luwum were sentenced to death by a military tribunal after a secret hearing in which legal representation was denied. Among them were the retired chairman of Uganda's Public Service Commission, the Assistant Commissioner of Labour, senior police officers and prison officials. On 9 September they were publicly executed, together with three other prisoners.

The absence of restraint on killings of political opponents and criminal suspects led to many other civilians being seized and killed by members of the security forces for criminal motives or quite arbitrarily. Many people were killed simply because a security officer or soldier wanted to take their wife, or seize their house, car, cattle or other property. It is likely that a substantial proportion of killings by the security forces were of this nature. These killings, however, were linked to the killing of political opponents in that any resistance to the order or demand of a security officer was taken as opposition to the government and a reason for killing. The "spoils system" of licensed theft and pillage was intended to ensure loyalty to the government from security agents and was condoned at the highest levels.

Most people arrested and killed on suspicion of having committed an offence regarded by the government as political or security-related were probably arrested on highly insubstantial evidence, such as the uncorroborated word of another security agent or an informer, and could not have been convicted if fairly tried. Journalists who examined Bureau of State Research documents after the fall of the Amin government noted how preposterous the allegations against prisoners were, and how absurd the records of interrogation–conducted under torture and the ever-present threat of death.

The government denied most of the killings, claimed that many people who had "disappeared" and been killed had left the country, and tried to place the responsibility for killings committed by security agents on "imperialists", "Zionist agents" or former President Obote's Tanzanian-based guerrillas. An independent commission of inquiry into the "disappearances" was established in 1974, but its findings were suppressed and no steps were taken to end the abuses. The commission's members later fled the country or suffered reprisals.

During the entire period of President Amin's government, no security official was charged, fairly tried, convicted and punished for any act of arbitrary arrest, illegal detention, torture or murder. The few actions that were taken against security commanders were designed either to deflect criticism without actually punishing the offender, or to remove (by killing) a person considered by President Amin as a threat to his position.

Human rights violations in Uganda were raised in inter-governmental forums several times between 1971 and 1979. In 1974 and 1976 the International Commission of Jurists made detailed submissions on Uganda to the United Nations Commission on Human Rights. The commission took no action in 1975 and President Amin announced that he had been exonerated from what he called a "smear campaign". In 1976 the Human Rights Commission's Sub-Commission on Prevention of Discrimination and Protection of Minorities recommended that the commission should undertake a thorough study of human rights violations in Uganda. By 1977 Uganda had secured a seat on the commission. When the commission met in February and March 1977, it reportedly decided to keep the situation under review but to take no further action. In 1977 the Commonwealth heads of government and the European Community foreign ministers issued statements deploring violations of human rights in Uganda. In 1978 the UN Commission on Human Rights reportedly authorized a special rapporteur to look into the human rights situation in Uganda.

President Amin's government was overthrown in April 1979 after the invasion of Uganda by the Tanzanian army and militia and small Ugandan guerrilla groups (the largest being Tanzanian-trained and loyal to Milton Obote). This followed an incursion into Tanzania by President Amin's troops. After a "transitional" 20-month period of two civilian and one virtually military government, elections in December 1980 returned former President Milton Obote to power.

In 1980 the UN Economic and Social Council and the UN Commission on Human Rights sought to encourage international assistance for Uganda to overcome the legacy of brutality and the destruction of the country's legal structure. The UN Secretary-General was asked in 1982 to help the Government of Uganda to take measures to guarantee human rights, for example, by assistance in revising Ugandan law in conformity with recognized human rights norms and in training for police and prison officers. However, Amnesty International was disturbed by numerous reports of renewed human rights violations in Uganda during 1981 and 1982, including killings by the army.

Argentina: 'disappearances' and extrajudicial executions

"Before getting out of the lorry, the prisoners were tied up. They were then taken from the lorry and were forced to kneel in front of the trenches and then they were shot. I believe that these assassinations became a sort of military ceremony. Captain González also said that sometimes the officer in charge of the firing-squad allowed the prisoners 'five minutes' to pray. Sometimes they were told that they were being executed for 'treason'. Those who were arrested while doing compulsory military service were shot wearing their uniform.

"The bodies, riddled with bullets, lay in the trenches. They were then covered with an inflammable substance and burned.

"Officers from all units of the III Army Corps witnessed the executions, from lieutenants to generals."
Testimony of Graciela Geuna, a prisoner in the secret La Perla *camp, Córdoba, Argentina, from 1976 to 1977.*

Since the March 1976 military coup the Argentine armed forces have killed many real or imagined opponents of the military government as part of a "war" against subversion. It is impossible to know the precise number of victims. This is partly because of the secrecy surrounding the "war" against subversion and partly because most of these killings have been bound to the practice of "disappearances" carried out by the armed forces after the coup. General Roberto Viola, Commander-in-chief of the army from 1976 to 1979 and later President, admitted in March 1981 that there were between 7,000 and 10,000 dead and "disappeared".

The term "disappearance" refers to political abductions carried out by the police, the security forces, or in some cases armed squads claiming public authority. Their prisoners then "disappear": friends and relatives are unable to establish their whereabouts or ascertain their fate.

After the 1976 coup abductions followed by "disappearance" virtually replaced formal arrest and imprisonment in political cases. There is ample evidence of victims of political killings having first been abducted by the security forces and taken to secret camps, then killed and their bodies dumped.

The secrecy surrounding "disappearances" has served to hide the scale of extrajudicial executions. Several hundred people are known to have been unlawfully killed by order of the government or with its complicity since the coup: at least 6,000 are known to have "disappeared".

The fate of the "disappeared" is the subject of agonized speculation and disquieting rumours. Relatives reject the suggestion that they are dead. Yet the Inter-American Commission on Human Rights of the Organization of American States (IACHR) in a 1980 report after a mission to Argentina drew "the painful conclusion that the great majority of the 'disappeared' persons have died through causes it is unable to determine exactly but which, in any event, entail a great responsibility for those who captured or detained them".

Killings by death squads before the 1976 coup

Political violence has marked Argentina's history for many years, both under civilian governments and under military rule. A state of siege was declared in 1969 after the violent suppression of an uprising by the armed forces, in which more than 20 civilians were killed. From 1970 onwards the activities of left-wing armed groups intensified, and further repressive legislation was passed.

In March 1973 elections were held and the Peronist candidate, Héctor Cámpora, became President. After 49 days in office he resigned and in September 1973 Juan Domingo Perón became President. President Perón was succeeded on his death in July 1974 by his widow, María Estela Martínez de Perón. In the following months political violence increased as factional fighting spread. On 6 November 1974 a state of siege was introduced and more than 3,000 people suspected of involvement in subversive activities were placed in preventive detention.

It was during 1973 that death squads and paramilitary right-wing gangs emerged. These groups directed organized violence against what could broadly be called the left — students, lawyers, journalists and trade unionists. Although unofficial, they would often act openly, claiming responsibility for their actions and inflicting punishments as a means of intimidation. These groups operated with impunity and were responsible for a large proportion of the approximately 1,500 assassinations which occurred in the 18 months following President Perón's death.

One of the first groups to operate was the *Alianza Anti-comunista Argentina* (AAA), the Argentine Anti-Communist Alliance. Between June and December 1973 this organization was almost certainly responsible for 29 killings. In Córdoba another group came into being: the *Comando Libertadores de América*, Liberators of America Commando, which had close links with the armed forces. The *Comando's* first act was a raid on a student hostel and the murder of six Bolivian students, none of whom had any political connections. Later attacks were clearly designed not just to kill "leftists" but to instill terror. It was on this group's initiative that secret camps were first established in the province of Córdoba.

There is evidence that the authorities did more than simply tolerate the death squads. The *Comando Libertadores*, for instance, was composed of junior-ranking army officers. Evidence of high-level involvement with the death squads was provided by a former official of the Ministry of Social Welfare, Salvador Paino. A congressional commission of inquiry in February 1976 investigated the activities of the former Minister of Social Welfare, José López Rega. In sworn statements Salvador Paino revealed that the former Minister had been one of the founders of the AAA and had used the Ministry's press attaché as an intermediary between himself and the group.

Neither before nor after the 1976 coup were the crimes of the death squads investigated.

The coup and its aftermath

On 24 March 1976 President María Estela de Perón was deposed by the armed forces, who promised to provide economic stability and to wage a total "war" against subversion. In the view of the armed forces subversion was a sinister and pervasive threat, a threat that could be overcome only by a pervasive counter-attack. General Jorge Rafael Videla, who became President after the coup, affirmed: "A terrorist is not just someone with a gun or bomb but also someone who spreads ideas that are contrary to Western and Christian civilization." For the commanding officers it was not enough to root out known subversives; they identified the enemy, in a much broader sense, as a left-wing or seditious mentality. Success required a rounding up of all suspects, extensive inquiries and interrogations, a total elimination of those believed to be dangerous. In their view, an amnesty granted to political prisoners in 1973 had allowed former prisoners to resume guerrilla activities — more permanent solutions were required.

However, openly violent practices were to be avoided. They had learned from the Chilean experience in which the brutality of early repressive measures had earned the Pinochet government international condemnation. Just as the possibility of prisoners being released was to be avoided, so it was advisable to act in secret.

After the coup, national institutions were rapidly militarized and political power concentrated in the hands of the military *junta*, which nominated the President and the governors of the provinces. The *junta* dissolved Congress indefinitely and replaced all members of the Supreme Court as well as the Attorney General with military appointees. The state of siege introduced in 1974 continued and even its minimal safeguards were violated. Constitutional guarantees were further curtailed. Extensive exceptional legislation was passed, giving the armed forces virtually unlimited powers. Suspects could be detained indefinitely or dealt with summarily by military tribunals; the death penalty, abolished in 1972, was reintroduced and the age of criminal responsibility was reduced to 16 years.

Alongside the exceptional legislation enacted after the coup there appears to have existed a secret repressive structure under the aegis of the Commanders-in-chief of the armed forces. Written orders authorizing its implementation have never been published but in a number of speeches by high-ranking army officers reference has been made to their existence: "We waged war with the doctrine in hand, with written orders from the Superior Commands, we never needed paramilitary organizations." (General Santiago Omar Riveros, quoted by the IACHR, 1980.) The influential retired army general, General Tomas Sánchez de Bustamante, has described the methods used to tackle subversion: "In this kind of struggle, the secrecy that must surround the operations means that not even the name of a prisoner or wanted person should be divulged; a cloud of silence must encompass everything and this is not compatible with freedom of the press. Neither is ordinary justice compatible with the speed and gravity with which such cases must be judged."

Under this secret counterpart to the legal structure anti-subversive operations were decentralized and made the direct responsibility of each regional army commander. Task forces or command units were established drawing men from all branches of the armed forces. In Buenos Aires the navy assumed responsibility for actions in the northern sector of the city, with the *Escuela de Mecánica de la Armada*, Navy Mechanics School, as its operations base. The air force largely controlled activities in the provinces of Mendoza and San Luis. This jurisdiction was not always accepted

54

since rivalry between the forces was great. The command units within each area had complete autonomy from the ordinary police and military chain of command, just as their regional commanders had autonomy, in anti-subversive operations, from their superior officers, the President, his cabinet, and the judiciary.

In Córdoba, for example, anti-subversive operations were carried out by the *Destacamento 141 de Inteligencia General Iribarren*, Intelligence Unit Number 141. This unit was under the direct control of the Third Army Corps, which received detailed weekly reports. Command of the unit was in the hands of an army colonel and his deputy, a lieutenant colonel. From the unit's base four sectors were controlled: the "political" sector, the operations squad, a secret camp known as *La Perla* or OP3 (run by a captain and a lieutenant), and the logistics sector. Investigations were carried out by the operations squad but priorities in investigation were set by the political sector. The political sector also controlled all high-level contacts. Information, including that obtained in *La Perla*, was processed by the political sector and then sent to intelligence headquarters in the capital, Buenos Aires. The political sector also decided which prisoners should be released and in which cases custody should be acknowledged.

The keynote of the extra-legal methods used by the security forces was "disappearance". Although those carrying out these secret actions had a certain autonomy, the view that the overall responsibility lay with the Armed Forces High Command was clearly stated in the IACHR's conclusion to its report on Argentina: "The Commission is morally convinced that, in general, these authorities could not have been ignorant of the events as they were occurring and did not adopt the necessary measures to terminate them."

For a short time after the coup the methods of the pre-coup death squads persisted, and a number of deliberately horrifying killings were perpetrated, some of them ostensibly in retaliation for killings by guerrillas. After the assassination in August 1976 of General Omar Actis, the head of the state committee organizing the World Cup, 30 bullet-ridden and dynamited bodies were found near the town of Pilar outside Buenos Aires. Near the bodies a placard had been left with the words "Montoneros cemetery", a reference to one of the left-wing revolutionary organizations. All the victims were young, and police did not allow relatives of missing people to see the bodies. According to a recent statement given to Amnesty International, the victims had been removed from Federal Police Headquarters in Buenos Aires on the orders of the Head of the Tactical Department and shot. Their bodies were buried in a common grave in the Derqui Cemetery.

Before 1976 many people suspected of involvement with revolutionary organizations had been imprisoned. After the coup, arrest and official imprisonment of political suspects gave way to "disappearances". Typically, the victims were dragged from their houses at night by men who identified themselves as agents of the police or the armed forces. When relatives tried to find out what had happened to them, they received no information or help. The arrests might be acknowledged and the prisoners might even be released after a brief period in detention, but usually they were taken to secret camps belonging to the armed forces or the police, not officially recognized prisons. Almost all were tortured and the majority have never been seen again. Between the coup in 1976 and the end of 1979 at least 6,000 people "disappeared".

Deaths in custody

At the time of the coup there were about 3,000 political prisoners in Argentina. Some prisoners were suspected of involvement with left-wing revolutionary groups which had carried out armed assaults and kidnappings during the Peronist government. In December 1975 all prisons had been placed under military jurisdiction, and conditions deteriorated immediately after the coup. Political prisoners in Córdoba, Coronda, Resistencia and Salta were denied all contact with the outside world for over six months. Visits by lawyers ceased for all prisoners detained at the disposal of the executive power (held indefinitely without being charged). Lists of prisoners were not published and the authorities refused to state exactly how many people were in detention. The International Committee of the Red Cross was unable to visit official prisons. During this period a series of killings of political prisoners occurred. In Córdoba Penitentiary, for example, where some 400 prisoners were held, 25 political prisoners met violent deaths between 17 May and 18 October 1976. Prisoners smuggled out a letter to Cardinal Primatesta of Córdoba asking for his intervention to protect the lives of the remaining prisoners after a group of six had been killed. The following account is based on the testimonies of political prisoners in Córdoba Penitentiary:

"On 17 May 1976 the following were removed from the jail without any explanation: Miguel Angel Mosse, Ricardo Alberto Otto Young, Alberto Svaguzza, Eduardo Alberto Hernández, Luis Ricardo Verón and Diana Fidelman. Minutes later they were killed; the army alleged they were shot while trying to escape.

"On 28 May José A. Pucheta and Carlos Sgandurra were taken out of their cells and killed (allegedly killed during a rescue attempt).

"On 19 June at 23.15 hours while we were all sleeping Mirta Abdón de Maggi and Esther Barneris were taken away, gagged, handcuffed and blindfolded. The same night, they took Miguel Barreras and Claudio Zorrilla. All were subsequently shot with other detainees who were not from the prison (once again the official version was 'shot during an escape attempt').

"On 5 July, during one of the infamous 'dances' while doing press-ups, prisoner Raúl Augusto Bauducco unintentionally touched the officer in charge, who shot him dead. (The official statement was that the prisoner had tried to snatch the officer's gun.)"

Four more political prisoners died in the Córdoba Penitentiary in mid-October 1976. Death notices were published in the local newspaper *Voz del Interior* (15 October and 18 October 1976) for Miguel Angel Cevallos, Jorge Oscar García, Pablo Alberto Ballustra and Marta Juana González de Baronetto.

A number of political prisoners in other prisons were killed in similar circumstances during 1976 and 1977. These deaths had a number of factors in common: the victims appear to have been selected on the basis of their known connection with revolutionary groups; all died in dubious circumstances; official explanations for the deaths were remarkably similar, referring to escape attempts. Prisoners being transferred were normally handcuffed, hooded and locked in cellular vans, and travelled under a heavily armed escort; any escape attempt would therefore appear to have been doomed to failure. None of the deaths was investigated further and newspapers were only permitted to print the official communiques about the incidents.

There were also people known to have been officially detained who, months later, were reported by the authorities as having been killed in clashes with security forces.

The fate of the 'disappeared'

What has become of the "disappeared" prisoners is one of the most sensitive questions in Argentine politics. Despite pressure, the armed forces have refused to publish lists of the dead or missing. Instead, relatives have been advised to consider the "disappeared" as "absent forever".

The fact that some long-term "disappeared" prisoners were eventually released has given rise to hopes that others may still be alive. There have been constant rumours, but little evidence, about the existence of camps in remote parts of the country. By the beginning of 1977 the location of virtually all the main secret centres of detention was known; the names of many had been published abroad.

In their testimonies, survivors of the secret camps described the regular "transfers" which took place. At first they believed that the prisoners were being released or moved to other camps or to official prisons. In some cases, this did indeed happen. But gradually they pieced together bits of information which led them to the conclusion that for most the "transfer" meant death.

Before deciding on who was to be transferred, camp officials would complete a form evaluating the political involvement of the individual and assessing whether the person concerned was "dangerous" or "potentially dangerous".

Testimony published in Madrid during 1981 described the system at the *Escuela de Mecánica de la Armada:*

"Prisoners had to remain in their cells in silence. At approximately 5 pm each Wednesday people were selected for the transfer. They were led one by one to the infirmary just as they were, dressed or half-dressed, in hot or cold weather. In the infirmary they were given an injection allegedly because 'hygiene' conditions in the camps they were going to were poor. In reality they were given a kind of sedative. Then they were taken by lorry to the *Aeroparque* (a military airfield) in Buenos Aires, near the ESMA, and put on a Fokker airplane belonging to the navy's multi-purpose air squadron. They would be flown out to sea towards the south to the point where the Gulf Stream would ensure the disappearance of the bodies. Then the prisoners were thrown alive out of the planes."

In Córdoba the system was slightly different. According to testimony by Graciela Geuna, a prisoner in the secret *La Perla* camp:

"Transfers of prisoners were common. They usually took place in lorries but occasionally cars were used. Prisoners who were 'transferred' by car were taken to *La Ribera* camp and were then released or sent to an official jail. In the second type of 'transfer', by lorry, comments made by

members of Intelligence Unit No. 141 indicated that the fate
of the transferred person was death by firing squad, in the
countryside near *La Perla*...

"At first 20 or more prisoners were transferred together,
each day. Later the number fell to about three. I
subsequently learned that the lorry was driven to a field
between two main roads (Carlos Paz and La Calera). The
place was close to *La Perla* because after about 20 minutes
we could hear the lorry returning, presumably to report on
the operation.

"From Captain González I later learned that when the
lorry reached the chosen spot the graves had already been
dug."

These allegations have provoked much controversy and grief in
Argentina. Some Argentines believe that these testimonies have
been manufactured by the intelligence services to undermine the
morale of the families of "disappeared" prisoners. Others, conced-
ing that they may be true, feel that such statements should not be
published and that efforts on behalf of "disappeared" prisoners
should proceed on the premise that all are alive until the government accounts for them.

Coastguards in Argentina and Uruguay have corroborated
certain allegations. Victor González del Río, then a member of the
Argentine coastguard, had to deal with the cases of 10 corpses that
were washed ashore between 1977 and 1979 during the bathing
season in Punta Norte and Punta Sur. He later told Amnesty
International:

"You could see that it was not a normal drowning. The
attitudes of drowned people show that they fought against
the sea; you saw the despair on their faces. In these cases,
however, they were probably already dead or unconscious at
the time when they were thrown into the sea.

"The dead bodies were, so far as one could see, in the
30-year-old group. The corpses were usually mutilated by the
fish. I think that they had been drifting in the sea from a few
days up to a few weeks. A number of corpses showed traces
of ill-treatment, such as severed hands. Most corpses were
naked, without rings, watches or necklaces. Sometimes they
wore underwear and in one case the body had been packed
in a nylon bag.

"The police then let me know in guarded terms that I had to
keep my mouth shut about this. They also suggested that the

corpses had probably come from wrecked fishing boats. But reports of wrecked fishing boats had never reached me."

The Inter-American Commission on Human Rights visited public cemeteries, examined unmarked graves and inspected cemetery registers during its 1980 mission to Argentina. It received information that members of the armed forces had entered the graveyards during the night to bury corpses. In its examination at *La Plata* cemetery, the commission found that most of those buried in unmarked graves were between 20 and 30 years old. In all cases a doctor had helped draw up a death certificate. In most of the 102 cases that had been registered between 1976 and 1979, the cause of death was given as "destruction of the brain by a firearm projectile". The commission advised the Argentine authorities that, when deaths occur in confrontations between state forces and groups classified by the government as subversive, a full report should be prepared giving the place, time and circumstances of the hostilities and other information about the number and identity of those killed.

In 1979 a change of policy could be discerned. Although "disappearances" continued to be reported — 30 cases were reported in 1980 — abductions appeared to be more selective. Those seized had a greater chance of being released even though they were invariably tortured. This was the outcome in six of the 10 cases which occurred in 1981. But the killing of Horacio Alberto Castro in April 1981, two days after he was taken from his home by federal police officers, showed that the danger to life still remained. The motive for the killing would appear to have been his former connection to the small left-wing party, the *Partido Socialista de los Trabajadores* (PST), Socialist Workers Party. In three other cases the victims remain "disappeared".

On the evening of 4 February 1982 Ana María Martínez, who worked in the northwest zone of Greater Buenos Aires, left her home to do some shopping locally. At about 8.30 pm she was abducted on the corner of the street where she lived. According to witnesses, she was forced into an olive green Ford Falcon car by an armed man and woman. The car was then driven away at high speed. Those who witnessed the incident made no attempt to intervene because of the speed with which it was carried out and because the abductors were armed. However, one witness later made a complaint to the local police pointing out that a similar car had been stationed outside the house of Ana María Martínez throughout the previous day, 3 February. The car had been occupied by two people — a man and a woman. The local police refused to look into the complaint.

On 9 February 1982 a writ of *habeas corpus* was presented to Federal Court No. 2 in San Martín. The court passed on the information the same day to the Minister of the Interior and to the security forces. The following day, 10 February, a delegation of lawyers went to various police stations and offices in the area to make inquiries.

On 17 February 1982 the Minister of the Interior announced that Ana María Martínez' body had been found in the suburbs of Buenos Aires. Her body had, in fact, been found buried on 12 February and was not identified until 17 February.

At the time of her abduction, Ana María Martínez was three months pregnant. She had been active in trade union work and had been a sympathizer of the PST.

To date the Argentine Government has shown itself unwilling to clarify the question of the "disappeared" perhaps in the hope that their silence would discourage further investigation and the problem would be forgotten. However, relatives of the victims are pledged to continue to seek clarification and accountability from the authorities and are unlikely to abandon their efforts. The discovery of unmarked graves in October 1982 in a number of cemeteries has only served to highlight the question once again and to demonstrate that it must be confronted and not forgotten.

'Encounter' killings in India

"I was taken to Mulug police station.... In the evening at about 8.00 pm [24 July 1975] the police came.... We [witness and four others] were all put into the police van.... We were taken into the midst of the forest.... We were made to get down from the van and we were taken about a mile to walk.... Then the [Sub-Inspector] addressed me 'at least even now divulge the truth' .... I was kept there. The remaining four people were taken to a distance of 50 feet and were tied to trees by ropes from foot to chest, with the handcuffs on. A black cloth was tied over my eyes. The other four were also blindfolded. I heard S.P. directing to fire. I heard one of them refusing to 'fire'. Thereupon S.P. abused him in English. The people who were tied were raising slogans — 'Long live Mao, Long live the Revolution'. I heard the firing of guns six times.... Then S.R. approached me and said 'you bastard you are lucky you are still alive'.... I was still blindfolded.... After I was put into the van my blindfold was removed and I happened to look out and I found those four people with their heads hanging. Then I saw their ropes being removed and the four dead bodies were taken away in a jeep.... I was warned not to disclose this incident to anybody otherwise I will be shot dead like the other four...."
Testimony submitted to the official Bhargawa commission of inquiry into "encounter" killings in Andhra Pradesh.

Since the inception of the "Naxalite" movement in India in the late 1960s, many alleged Naxalites (members of the Communist Party of India (Marxist-Leninist)) have been killed by police in what many Indians believe are staged incidents. There is even a special term for such incidents: the police say that "extremists" were killed in "encounters" with the police. Some Indian newspapers simply refer to "encounter killings". Other frequently given official explanations are that prisoners were killed while "trying to escape from prison" or while "resisting arrest".

The killing of political suspects follows an earlier established practice of killing suspected dacoits (robbers). (Dacoity is robbery in which five or more people are involved.) Meherchand Mahajan, a former Chief Justice and Head of the Punjab Police Commission, established by the Indian Government in 1961 to inquire into allegations that criminal suspects were being killed in staged "encounters" with the police, stated that:

> "Considerable evidence has been led to the effect that police make out false encounters with criminals and shoot them because they cannot obtain sufficient evidence against them to bring them to justice before the courts of law.... A number of witnesses ... suggested that when the police catch hold of dacoits and can obtain no evidence against them, they tie them to trees and just liquidate them."

The central government's response to expressions of concern about "encounter" killings has invariably been to deny responsibility on the ground that under the Indian Constitution law and order was a subject for state authorities. In rare cases where the Indian Government has prompted state governments to establish judicial inquiries into "encounter" killings, it has failed to take action when state authorities subsequently frustrated and curtailed the inquiries. The central government's lack of determination to establish inquiries into "encounter" killings, or to pursue the completion of inquiries when they have been set up, demonstrates a degree of acquiescence in such killings. This is particularly so where reports of "encounter" killings have been persistently put forward for many years, and have been investigated and described in detail by authoritative civil liberties organizations within India.

'Encounter' killings of Naxalites

The Communist Party of India (Marxist-Leninist) was formed in 1969 after a split from the Communist Party of India (Marxist). Its members followed the policy advocated by one of the party's leaders in 1967 of "annihilating class enemies". Their aim was to bring about rapid social and economic change against the background of poverty and unemployment prevailing in many Indian states. Landlords and police officers were selected for attack, particularly in the late 1960s in Andhra Pradesh and in West Bengal in the early 1970s, when these violent tactics caused the death of many police officers in Calcutta. Reports that Naxalites had been killed in "encounters" with the police began to appear in the press.

During a 1978 mission to Indian Amnesty International interviewed

Shambynath Shaha, an alleged Naxalite, who had survived an "encounter" attack and still showed the marks of five bullet wounds. His account is typical of such incidents. Shambynath Shaha was arrested on 16 November 1970 by the Calcutta police, taken to Lal Bazar police station, asked the names and hiding places of Naxalites, and tortured. He was then taken, handcuffed, by police to Salt Lake outside Calcutta. He was ordered to walk away from the car and was shot three times at close range. Still alive, he was taken to the bank of the Ganges, where another three shots were fired, two of which hit him. Unconscious, he was taken to a third place and shot at once more. He was taken to Marwari Relief Society Hospital, where the next morning the police came to collect his body and the death certificate. But he had been operated upon and survived. The police alleged that he received the wounds in an "encounter" on the morning of 17 November 1970, one day after his arrest.

Since 1968 killings of left-wing "extremists" in "encounters" with the police or "while trying to escape" have been reported from eight of the 22 Indian states: Andhra Pradesh, West Bengal, Orissa, Punjab, Bihar, Kerala, Tamil Nadu and Maharashtra. On 17 December 1980 India's Minister of State for Home Affairs, Yogendra Makwana, stated in a written reply in the *Lok Sabha* (the lower house of the Indian parliament) that 216 Naxalites had been killed in Andhra Pradesh in "police firings" since 1968, adding that the firings were "a sequel to armed attacks launched by Naxalites on police". The Minister acknowledged that similar "encounters" had taken place in Maharashtra, Tripura and Tamil Nadu.

Legislation facilitating 'encounter' killings

The most detailed information about "encounter" killings has come from the state of Andhra Pradesh, where the Naxalite movement gained support among tribal people in the Srikakulam district, living in poor conditions and often landless. During 1968 and 1969 the Naxalites singled out landlords and police officers for "selective assassination". The government responded by reviving the 1948 Madras Suppression of Disturbances Act, and the state of Andhra Pradesh declared certain areas "Disturbed Areas" by simple notification in the government Gazette.

The act provides that in "Disturbed Areas" certain offences under the Indian Penal Code, which are normally punishable with imprisonment, can be punished with death. Aiding or abetting such offences may also incur the death penalty. Furthermore, a Sub-Inspector of Police has powers to shoot if in his opinion an assembly of more than five people is unlawful, or if people are found carrying weapons or things capable of being used as weapons.

Article 5 of the act reads:

"Any magistrate and any Police Officer not below the rank of Sub-Inspector may, if in his opinion it is necessary to do so for restoring or maintaining public order, after giving such warning, if any, as he may consider necessary, *fire upon, order fire to be opened or otherwise use force, even to the causing of death*, against any person who in a disturbed area is acting in contravention of any law or order for the time being in force in such area, prohibiting the assembly of five or more persons or the carrying of weapons or of things capable of being used as weapons." (Emphasis added)

Andhra Pradesh lawyers have told Amnesty International that people caught in urban areas had been taken to "Disturbed Areas" so that the shootings could "be put beyond the pale of the law". They say that many of the tribal population normally carry bows and arrows but that police reports (in India called "First Information Reports") have depicted these weapons as being used against the police.

Section 6 of the act gives the police immunity from prosecution or any other form of legal proceedings, "except with the previous sanction of the Provincial Government". The act has been in force in certain areas of the state for more than 10 years and is widely believed to have facilitated the shooting of suspected political activists by the police after arrest.

Official and unofficial inquiries

After the 1975–1977 state of emergency interest in the protection of human rights in India increased; civil liberties organizations were established in many states to investigate human rights abuses which had occurred during and before the emergency. Several of them investigated reports of "encounter" killings.

In Andhra Pradesh an unofficial inquiry committee headed by the President of the Supreme Court Bar Association, Mr Tarkunde, investigated the cases of 19 people officially stated to have died in "encounters" in 1975 and 1976. It concluded that the "encounters" in three cases did not take place at all, that there were serious doubts about the fourth "encounter" and that all 19 people had in fact been shot in cold blood by the police, some of them after severe torture. The names of police officials involved were submitted to the Union Home Minister.

In June 1977 members of the Indian parliament demanded an inquiry into the allegations of the Tarkunde committee and the Andhra Pradesh government established a judicial inquiry headed by Justice Bhargawa.

The Bhargawa Commission is the only example in India of an official judicial inquiry established to investigate, on a statewide basis, allegations that political activists apprehended by the police were killed in staged "encounters". Its terms of reference included:

"–the facts and circumstances in regard to each one of the encounters between police and the so-called Naxalites during the period 1968 to 1977

–the allegations of murder, torture and brutal treatment of Naxalite prisoners

–the administrative measures required to deal with that problem in the future."

There was much criticism in the Andhra Pradesh state assembly that the terms of reference of the commission did not include an investigation of responsibility for the killings. The opposition asked for the police personnel responsible to be named.

The Bhargawa Commission, which started in September 1977, was not successful. Lawyers appearing before the commission told Amnesty International that witnesses who had earlier testified before the unofficial Tarkunde committee were intimidated by the police and had even been arrested when on their way to testify before the commission. They stated that of the 21 witnesses scheduled to appear, 12 were "taken away" by the police or otherwise prevented from appearing. Police records were allegedly interfered with and records of arrest were not kept in "encounter" cases. Proceedings before the commission showed that police formalities (such as registering identification marks of those arrested) were not followed in the cases of people killed in "encounters".

In June 1978 the Andhra Pradesh government ordered the commission to hold proceedings *in camera* "in the public interest", to ensure that the administration and the police were not "discredited". The Andhra Pradesh government refused to extend the time limit for the commission to submit its report beyond 30 June 1978, and in the face of these decisions, the commission terminated its work without submitting a report.

Commenting on the failure of the Bhargawa Commission to complete its inquiries Mr. Tarkunde, who had headed the earlier unofficial inquiry, said:

> "The conduct of the Andhra Pradesh government in relation to the Bhargawa Commission has shown that commissions appointed by the state government–when conduct of the state government is being inquired into–will be gravely hampered by the state government itself."

In the Punjab, the Punjab Civil Rights Committee investigated the deaths of eight Naxalites between 1970 and 1976. In all eight cases the official explanation had been that the victims were Naxalites killed in "encounters" by the police, but the committee received evidence from people who said that they had seen the victims being arrested, or had seen them in custody or being taken to the spot where they were killed. The committee concluded that each of the eight men had been "murdered by the police". Two men had been tortured before being shot, two others died of torture, and the other four were shot shortly after being apprehended.

The Punjab committee pointed in its 1978 interim report to the lack of government investigation of the eight cases:

> "In each of the instances, relatives and associates of the victims as well as other residents of the villages petitioned various levels of the State and Central Government (including the Prime Minister) urging them to institute judicial inquiries. In each case the requests were turned down."

Recent cases

Although the Naxalite movement is today split into several factions, and the "annihilation policy" has been abandoned by most, press reports in recent years have mentioned a few incidents of alleged killings of landlords and other "class enemies" by Naxalites in Kerala, Tamil Nadu and Andhra Pradesh. A number of "encounter" killings of Naxalites in recent years have also been reported: three Naxalites reportedly killed in September 1981 in Bihar; 10 young men alleged to have died in "encounters" in Andhra Pradesh between October 1980 and April 1982, most following torture; 13 alleged Naxalites killed in Tamil Nadu between August and December 1980.

The series of 13 killings of Naxalites in the Tirupattur area of North Arcot, Tamil Nadu, began on 6 August 1980 when a bomb explosion killed three police officers escorting a Naxalite leader. The police version of this and the subsequent 12 killings, according to the Indian newspaper *The Statesman*, was that "they were flushed out of the forests in the Yellagiri hills, where they were hiding". But *The Statesman* reported that "several of them, far from being in hiding, were working openly as trade union leaders", and that evidence suggested that almost all of the 13 were killed after being arrested in towns and villages. One of the 13, Kanakraj, was "killed on September 18 in an encounter with the police when he was attempting to throw a bomb" according to press reports. But *The Statesman*, investigating earlier reports on the killings by a civil liberties organization, reported that "there are people who saw him being arrested while he was reading a newspaper in a teashop ....He was taken to Kalkathiyur village and shot." Another Naxalite, Kannamani, was "killed in a gun battle" according to the police. But according to *The Statesman*:

"There are people who saw the police seizing Kannamani while he was working on a road .... His hands were tied .... and he demanded that he should be produced before a magistrate .... He was taken instead to the police station.... A local crime reporter who happened to be at the police station at that time told *The Statesman* correspondent that Kannamani was threatened with a knife.... Finally he was made to stand facing the wall and was shot according to the people of the area."

The Chief Minister of Tamil Nadu refused to discuss these cases with *The Statesman* correspondent. Other attempts to investigate the cases have been resisted by the police: members of a civil liberties organization travelling to the area in October 1980 were beaten up and their notes taken away by the police. Local journalists have been discouraged from investigating the allegations.

On 28 March 1981 the Tamil Nadu Finance Minister denied opposition charges that Naxalites had been shot dead deliberately by police in the Tirupattur area of North Arcot. "If any specific instance was brought to its notice, suitable action would be taken", he said. However, the state government has not responded to several demands by local civil liberties groups that judicial inquiries be established to investigate the circumstances of the deaths.

Conclusions

Given the failure of state governments to pursue inquiries and take measures to prevent staged "encounter" killings, the central government should itself establish an independent judicial mechanism for the entire country, to which complaints of this nature can be brought, and should not leave it to state governments to establish inquiries. A central government body could follow up investigations and see to it that appropriate measures are taken against individual police officers against whom *prima facie* evidence of involvement has emerged, in line with Articles 9 and 10 of the UN Declaration against Torture.

The success of such measures will continue to depend on the extent to which local civil liberties groups, lawyers and journalists are willing to investigate and report on illegal killings by the police, and the degree to which politicians and others are willing to press consistently for police reform.

There are detailed provisions against torture in the Indian Constitution itself. These, and the Code of Conduct for Law Enforcement Officials, could be made part of routine police training methods, which should emphasize the obligation of each police officer to comply with formalities for arrest and detention — including the obligation to produce a detainee before a magistrate within 24 hours — in each case.

Legislation facilitating "encounter" killings such as the Andhra Pradesh Suppression of Disturbances Act and the Armed Forces (Special Powers) Act, 1958, should be abolished.

Libya: killings of 'enemies of the revolution'

"The counter-revolutionary forces may continue to work against the revolution despite the fact that they have been disarmed and their political, economic and social weapons have been taken away. In this case physical liquidation becomes inevitable....

"They have allied themselves with the enemies; with the international right wing, with colonialism, Zionism and reaction. They are still carrying out acts which are hostile to the revolution. Therefore, the revolutionary committees said: No. Physical liquidation for the enemies abroad should be carried out. This is what the revolutionary committees declared. Since then, the revolutionary committees have embarked on the physical liquidation of the enemies of the revolution abroad....

"The counter-revolutionary forces should be physically liquidated. The revolutionary task will not end unless the opposition is liquidated. This is not only applied to those who are abroad, but to all counter-revolutionary forces ...."

Excerpts from a speech by Colonel Mu'ammar Gaddafi to students at Al Fatih University on 10 May 1980.

In February 1980 the Third Congress of the Libyan Revolutionary Committees issued a declaration calling for the "physical liquidation" of enemies of the 1969 revolution living abroad, and of counter-revolutionary elements within Libya. Since then at least 14 Libyan citizens have been killed or wounded in assassination attempts in the Federal Republic of Germany, Greece, Italy, Lebanon, Great Britain and the United States of America.

Assassination attempts abroad

CASE I: Salem Rtemi
Personal details: Businessman living in Italy.
Circumstances: Disappeared in February 1980. Bullet-ridden body found in Rome in the boot of his car on 21 March.

Action by "host" government: Libyan suspect arrested by Italian police. No further information.
Reaction of Libyan authorities: Unknown.

CASE II: Muhammad Mustapha Ramadan
Personal details: 40, journalist, believed to be a Muslim activist. An exile from Libya since 1975. Openly critical of Gaddafi's regime.
Circumstances: 11 April 1980, London; shot dead after Friday's prayers outside Mosque in Regent's Park; received warning three days before killing.
Action by "host" government: Two Libyan suspects were detained, tried in September 1980, charged with murder and sentenced to life imprisonment. At trial they said that their victim had been sentenced to death by a revolutionary committee and they had taken it upon themselves to execute the sentence.
Reaction of Libyan authorities: Refused to allow Ramadan's body to be buried in Libya. Libyan airport authorities returned it to London.

CASE III: Abduljalil Aref
Personal details: 50, businessman living in Italy.
Circumstances: 19 April 1980, Rome. Shot in the head in a cafe in via Veneto.
Action by "host" government: Unknown.
Reaction of Libyan authorities: Shortly after killing, the Press Attaché of the people's bureau in Rome said "a traitor's list had been sent from Tripoli with the names of foreign-based opponents of Colonel Gaddafi."

CASE IV: Abdullatif Muntasser
Personal details: Relative of opposition leader Omar Al Muheisi.
Circumstances: 21 April 1980, shot dead, Beirut.
Action by "host" government: Unknown.
Reaction of Libyan authorities: Unknown.

CASE V: Mahmoud Abdul Salam Nafi'
Personal details: 40, lawyer, left Libya in 1969. Believed to be in contact with opposition groups but was also known to be a supporter of Colonel Gaddafi.
Circumstances: 25 April 1980, London. Shot dead in his office in Kensington.
Action by "host" government: Two Libyan suspects detained, charged with murder and tried September 1980. Sentenced to life imprisonment. At their trial they said that their victim had been sentenced to death by a revolutionary committee and they had

taken it upon themselves to execute the sentence.
Reaction of Libyan authorities: Unknown.

CASE VI: Abdallah Mohammad Al Khazmi
Personal details: 37, businessman.
Circumstances: Shot dead on 8 May 1980, Rome, in a cafe near the main railway station where he had an appointment with two other Libyans. One of the two men shot him at point-blank range.
Action by "host" government: Killers escaped.
Reaction of Libyan authorities: Refused to allow body to be buried in Libya.

CASE VII: Omran Al Mehddawi
Personal details: 43, former staff member of Libyan Embassy in Bonn. Living in exile after resigning from his post in 1978.
Circumstances: 10 May 1980, Bonn. Shot dead in the centre of the city.
Action by "host" government: Libyan suspect was arrested and sentenced to life imprisonment by a West German court on 22 December 1980. At trial defendant said that he had been sent by a revolutionary committee to act as executioner.
Reaction of Libyan authorities: Unknown.

CASE VIII: Mohammad Fouad Buhaggar
Personal details: Mid-50s, businessman, Libyan, with Tunisian nationality. Headed a Tunisian-based timber company with business in Rome.
Circumstances: 20 May 1980, Rome. Body found in a hotel room, knifed and strangled. A message in Arabic left in the room of the victim said: "God is great, the enemies of the people will be reached wherever they are. Long live the Libyan revolutionary committees in Rome."
Action by "host" government: Unknown.
Reaction of Libyan authorities: Unknown.

CASE IX: Abdul Rahman Bubaker
Personal details: Early 20s, factory worker. Known for his anti-Gaddafi views. Former army officer, left Libya in March 1980.
Circumstances: 21 May 1980, Athens. Found with his throat slit in his home in an Athens suburb. Inscription on wall was left behind: "The revolution will live forever. Death and no mercy to the imperialists."
Action by "host" government: Libyan suspect arrested, tried by Athens criminal court, convicted and sentenced to death. Sentence commuted to life imprisonment.
Reaction of Libyan authorities: Unknown.

CASE X: Salem Mohammad Fezzani

Personal details: Libyan-born but naturalized Italian, restaurant owner.

Circumstances: 21 May 1980, Rome, in his restaurant. Fezzani was shot at but escaped unhurt.

Action by "host" government: When arrested and charged with attempted murder the Libyan suspect, Merwin Belgassen Mansur, said: "I was sent by the Libyan people; he [Fezzani] is a traitor and an enemy of the people." The public prosecutor said that Mansur was sent to Italy with instructions to threaten selected fellow countrymen with death if they did not return to Libya. Mansur was sentenced to 15 years' imprisonment in January 1982 for attempted murder.

Reaction of Libyan authorities: Unknown.

CASE XI: Ezzedine Al Hodeiri

Personal details: 56, resident in the northern Italian town of Bolzano.

Circumstances: 11 June 1980, Milan. Shot dead in Central Milan Railway Station.

Action by "host" government: Unknown.

Reaction of Libyan authorities: Unknown.

CASE XII: Mohamed Saad Bekhit

Personal details: Early 30s.

Circumstances: 11 June 1980, Rome. Shot and injured but survived.

Action by "host" government: Suspect escaped.

Reaction of Libyan authorities: Unknown.

CASE XIII: Faisal Zagallai

Personal details: 35, student at Colorado State University, outspoken critic of Libyan regime. He was asked to return home and join the army about a year and a half before the attempt on his life but refused. Libyan Government stopped his scholarship. In May he reported a threat on his life to US authorities and was issued a permit for a gun. He had been resident in the USA for 10 years.

Circumstances: 14 October 1980, USA, in his home in Fort Collins, Colorado. He was shot and wounded (he lost an eye).

Action by "host" government: American suspect held, a 25-year-old veteran of Marines and US army who had links with Wilson, a former CIA agent then living in Libya. (Wilson has been charged in the USA with training terrorists and illegally exporting arms to Libya.) The suspect, Eugene Tafoya, was tried and sentenced in January 1982 to two years' imprisonment. At his trial he said that he was summoned to London to receive the Zagallai assignment, details of which were pushed under the door of his room in the Holiday Inn, London. He also admitted returning to London to be paid more than £4,210 for the job.

Reaction by Libyan authorities: The day after the shooting the Libyan news agency broadcast the following statement: "Confirming that physical liquidation is the final stage in the revolutionary dialectic, called for when economic, political and social weapons fail to put an end to the activities of counter-forces, a member of the international revolutionary committee has tried to liquidate one Faisal Zagallai, who was seriously wounded. Zagallai had studied at the expense of the [Libyan] community for 10 years at the American Colorado University to prepare for a master's degree and a doctorate. But instead of returning home to serve his country and people, he became an agent and a spy for American intelligence, supplying it with information about his country."

CASE XIV: Karim and Souad Kassuda
Personal details: Aged 7 and 8, children of Mr Farad Kassuda, 34, who refused to obey orders to return to Libya and was threatened. Living in exile in Portsmouth, UK.
Circumstances: 11 November 1980, Portsmouth. Children given poisoned peanuts by Libyan friend of family. Were gravely ill but survived.
Action by "host" government: Libyan suspect charged and tried in June 1981, received life imprisonment. He had allegedly said to Mr Kassuda when the latter refused to return to Libya: "You think we are joking but just you wait and see what happens to those who don't go back."
Reaction by Libyan authorities: Unknown.

CASE XV: Ahmed Mustapha Grea'a
Personal details: 32, student.
Circumstances: 29 November 1980, Manchester, UK. Stabbed to death in an apartment in Manchester.
Action by "host" government: Suspects flew back to Libya within hours of the killing.
Reaction by Libyan authorities: Unknown.

Background

March 1982 was the fifth anniversary of the establishment of "direct popular authority" as the basis of Libya's political system. In March 1977 Colonel Mu'ammar Gaddafi had declared his intention to create a society based on "direct democracy". All conventional forms of authority would be abandoned and direct people's power declared. Libya was renamed the Libyan Jamahiriya (People's Libya). This was followed by a series of steps to do away with the institutional structures of the state and its administration. To achieve direct rule by the people the Libyan population was divided into a series of bodies, such as people's congresses, people's committees, revolutionary committees and professional people's congresses (unions), all headed by the General People's Congress, the meeting place of the bodies' leading working groups.

Also in contrast to normal diplomatic relations, Libya would be represented in most parts of the world by "people's bureaux", rather than embassies. Colonel Gaddafi emphasizes that these are not embassies:

"We in Libya no longer deal with diplomatic matters in the traditional manner. We have people's congresses that hold authority. Abroad, we have people's bureaux which are considered the links between the people's congresses and other peoples of the world."

Colonel Gaddafi has stressed that relations between the People's Libyan Jamahiriya and other peoples must be a direct popular one through the people's bureaux:

"The members of the Libyan people's bureaux are unlike members of the diplomatic missions. They are free citizens, most of whom were Libyan students in those countries which now have bureaux. These students have marched on the embassies, turned them into people's bureaux and imposed the will of the masses."

By late 1979 the revolutionary committees, with the blessing of Colonel Gaddafi, had moved from "the area of motivation to the area of enforcement". These revolutionary committees can, in the words of the official text, "invite the masses to exercise their authority, agitate the popular congresses, lead the popular committees, to keep an eye on and eliminate the enemies of the revolution inside and abroad and generally propagate the revolution".

Calls for 'physical liquidation'

In February 1980 the Third Congress of the Libyan Revolutionary Committees issued a declaration which called *inter alia* for the "physical liquidation" of enemies of the revolution living abroad, and of elements within Libya considered to be obstructing "revolutionary change" in political or economic ways. The declaration was published by the official Libyan press *El Fajr Al Jadid* (New Dawn) and *Al Mu'allim* (The Teacher). The following is an unofficial translation of several passages in the declaration:

> "Physical liquidation is the final stage in the dialectic conflict between the revolution and its enemies, when all other means of liquidation (social, economic and political) have failed.

> "Issuing a last warning to the exploiting elements in previous contractors ... previous employers ... estate agents ... agents, and merchants to concentrate on production and to terminate their activities of exploitation and blackmail ... and their attempts to associate with revolutionary positions.

> "The liquidation of the elements that hinder the revolution from civilians to fascist and dictating military personnel ... traditionalists, dependent negativists and unproductive cowards that exploit power ... and those from the bourgeoisie who are parasites on the power of the revolution and on the people's authority."

In the months following this declaration, four Libyans in exile were sentenced to death in their absence by a revolutionary tribunal. In addition, hundreds of people were reported to have been arrested in Libya itself. Amnesty International has received reports that a number of those arrested died in custody: Amer Deghayes, a prominent lawyer and former Ba'athist leader in Libya, was arrested in late February 1980 and is reported to have died within days of his arrest.

During a mission to Libya between March and April 1980, Amnesty International delegates raised the issue of physical liquidation in talks with Libyan officials. Although acknowledging the call for physical liquidation, Libyan officials explained that according to the Third Universal Theory (Colonel Gaddafi's Green Book) the power was in the hands of the people themselves, and the people had therefore initiated the program of physical liquidation. It was merely an intimidatory measure, they insisted, which would not be implemented.

On 27 April 1980, however, Colonel Gaddafi announced that any Libyan living abroad who did not make immediate arrangements to return would be liquidated. On 28 April the official Libyan newspaper *El Zahaf El Akhdar* (The Green March) stated that the program of physical liquidation had begun to be

76

implemented and would not stop until all Libyans were back in their country. If they did not do so, the newspaper stated, there would be reprisals against their families in Libya, which would serve as an example to others.

The assassins

Since February 1980 there have been assassination attempts on Libyan citizens in Great Britain, the Federal Republic of Germany, the USA, Italy, Greece and the Lebanon. Fifteen such cases have been described in this chapter.

Most of the assassins have been Libyans, described in a number of cases as members of the "International Revolutionary Committees". From the evidence presented in court, they seem to have entered "host" countries as tourists or students shortly before they carried out the attacks. The weapons are believed to have been bought on the black market or to have been brought into the "host" country in diplomatic luggage.

In most cases the assassins have presented themselves as young zealots driven by faith rather than professional killers. They often described their victims as enemies of the revolution and the Libyan people. In several cases when Libyan suspects have been apprehended and tried abroad, they stated at their trial that their victims had been sentenced to death by a revolutionary committee, and that they had taken it upon themselves, or been sent, to execute the sentences.

The assailants' intention has been to kill their targets and to publicize the act. Most of the victims were shot at point-blank range in daylight in public places or at the home of the victim. The assassins often left slogans behind.

Reactions by 'host' governments

The measures taken by "host" governments have varied. In a number of cases suspects have been prosecuted in the courts of the "host" country. In other cases suspects have left the country or otherwise eluded the police. On occasion the "host" country has deported suspected members of assassination squads when evidence was not sufficient to justify an arrest warrant.

"Host" countries have also responded by extending police protection to Libyan dissidents thought to be possible targets and by increasing controls on Libyans entering the country. Checks at airports and other ports of entry have been tightened. "Host" countries have sent both public and personal protests to the Libyan Government. On occasion members of the Libyan people's bureaux have been expelled from the country when suspected of intimidating or threatening dissidents. One government has closed down Libya's mission and allowed only a special interest section to continue. The Libyans continue to insist that they have no embassies, or diplomatic representation, making it difficult to apply the well-established and almost universally accepted provisions of the Vienna Convention on diplomatic relations, which Libya ratified in 1977.

Colonel Gaddafi has explicitly sanctioned the international assassination campaign against his opponents in many official statements and press interviews. Several Libyan revolutionary bodies including revolutionary committees and people's bureaux have also reiterated their "determination to liquidate the enemies of the people's authority at home and abroad". On 10 October 1982 the Libyan news agency reported another speech by Colonel Gaddafi – this time to a meeting of basic people's congresses in Benghazi. He affirmed that the decision to liquidate "the remaining fugitives" must be taken by the Libyan people, publicly. The world must know about it, because what "would take place afterwards" would be the will of the people. Colonel Gaddafi stated that these people were "fugitives from justice working to tarnish Libya's reputation by means of the people's money which they had illegally transferred abroad".

78

The graves of Teodoro Aligado and Epifanio Simbajon, arrested without warrant by members of the Philippines Constabulary on 25 June 1981 in Barrio Lourdes, Pagadian City, Zamboanga del Sur province. They were taken on suspicion of being members of the New People's Army, the armed wing of the Communist Party of the Philippines. The two were removed from Pagadian City Jail on 29 June for further interrogation—later that day they were shot dead. Police officers alleged that they had been killed while trying to escape, but friends and relatives of the dead men have disputed the official version of events.

Libyan assassinated in London . . . police activity around the body of Mahmoud Abdul Salam Nafi', shot dead in the doorway of the Arab Legal Centre on 25 April 1980. The two Libyan gunmen who shot him were captured, tried for murder, convicted and sentenced to life imprisonment. At their trial they said that their victim had been sentenced to death by a revolutionary committee and they had taken it upon themselves to execute the sentences.

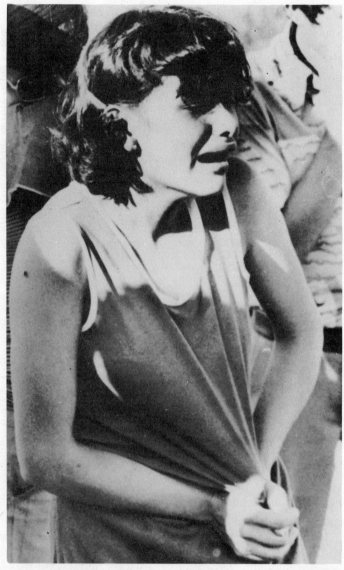

This women has just recognized her husband among the dead after the massacre of striking coffee plantation workers at El Porvenir, El Salvador, in early 1980. According to reports over 100 were killed by some 500 soldiers supported by tanks and helicopters.

Nearly 15,000 prisoners were killed here, at Tuol Sleng prison and execution centre ("S-21"), Phnom Penh, Kampuchea, between 1975 and 1979. Prison records show that on average 1,000 to 1,500 prisoners were held at any one time: most were tortured and forced to write confessions before being killed. On 15 October 1977, 418 people were killed; on 18 October the figure was 179; the highest single figure was 582 recorded executions on 27 May 1978.

Among the carved headstones in an Argentine graveyard outside Buenos Aires is a simple marker bearing the stencilled date of burial, 4 November 1976, and the two letters NN—*No Nombre*. No name. The burial places of many of the thousands of people who "disappeared" in the years after 1976 are marked in this way.

The body of a dead Guatemalan student lies on the ground . . . he was killed by armed men in an attack on the University of San Carlos on 4 July 1980. Government officials have denounced the university as a "centre of subversion" and staff and students have been killed. Between March and September 1980 at least 27 staff members were shot; the deaths continued in 1981 with the killings of the acting Dean of the Faculty of Law and six professors of law between 27 February and 7 May 1981.

One of several prison-execution grounds, at Khum Pra Phnom, Kampot Province, Kampuchea. Many such exhibits are officially displayed by the present government as a reminder of the atrocities committed under the rule of the former *Khmer Rouge* authorities. This photograph was taken in March 1983.

The funeral of Manuel Colom Argueta, former mayor of Guatemala City, machine-gunned to death in broad daylight in Guatemala City on 23 March 1979. His murder took place at a time when the centre-left political grouping of which he was a leading member was being granted official recognition which would allow it to contest elections. When his relatives presented the government with evidence of official involvement in the killing, they were charged with "calumny". One of his brothers and his sister were subsequently forced into exile after being followed and threatened by armed men.

86

Uganda, 1972. Troops of the Simba Batallion pose in front of a pile of corpses outside Simba Barracks, Kampala.

Killings at a school in San Salvador . . . a TV camera crew captured this grim sequence as a uniformed officer shoots two 15-year-old schoolboys, then turns and walks away. Both boys subsequently died. 26 June 1980.

International Legal Standards and Remedies

Extrajudicial executions are incompatible with existing standards of international law. On the most basic level, they violate the "right to life" articulated in all the fundamental international instruments on human rights. In addition, various categories of killings falling within the definition of extrajudicial executions are prohibited by more specific international legal provisions.

Despite this broad coverage of extrajudicial executions in international law, they have not until now been treated as a separate and distinct category of human rights violation towards which a common approach should be taken. The international community, in the forum of the United Nations, has only recently begun the conceptual process of linking the various sorts of killings which constitute extrajudicial executions. In 1980 the Sixth UN Congress on the Prevention of Crime and the Treatment of Offenders adopted a resolution deploring "extra-legal executions" which was an important first step in this process. (The UN uses the term "extra-legal executions" to refer to killings which would fall within Amnesty International's definition of extrajudicial executions.) It was followed by the UN General Assembly's adoption in 1980 and 1981 of resolutions relating to "arbitrary or summary executions". The UN Commission on Human Rights, in a resolution adopted in 1982, expressed deep alarm at "the occurrence of summary or arbitrary executions, including extra-legal executions" and called for the appointment of "a special rapporteur to examine the questions related to summary or arbitrary executions".

However, these resolutions and related initiatives taken in the UN have not managed to specify the types of killings to be encompassed. A clearer definition of extrajudicial executions in international law would be an important step in channelling the international community's current interest in the problem towards effective solutions.

Some machinery does already exist for the international community to react to extrajudicial executions. This machinery needs to be strengthened and augmented, however. A clarification of the concept of extrajudicial executions as a unique category of human rights violation in international law would assist the development of institutions and procedures specifically adapted to counter extrajudicial executions.

The right to life and standards for 'judicial' executions

The "right to life" is articulated in a number of basic international instruments on human rights.

The Universal Declaration of Human Rights states that "everyone has the right to life, liberty and security of person". The International Covenant on Civil and Political Rights (the "International Covenant"), the American Convention on Human Rights (the "American Convention") and the African Charter on Human and Peoples' Rights each specify that no individual shall be "arbitrarily" deprived of his or her life. The European Convention on Human Rights (the "European Convention") provides that "(n)o one shall be deprived of his life intentionally save in the execution of a sentence of a court following his conviction of a crime for which this penalty is provided by law". The International Covenant, the European Convention and the American Convention each state that the right to life "shall be protected by law". The common strand which emerges is that, to the extent that a government may deprive an individual of the right to life under the principles set out in these instruments, it must be only by a process which is "legal" and not arbitrary.

The International Covenant and the American Convention prescribe rules to be applied in death penalty cases. They both state that a death sentence may be imposed only for the most serious crimes. It can only be passed if a law laying down the death penalty as a punishment for that crime was in force before the crime was committed. Anyone sentenced to death has the right to seek pardon or commutation of the sentence. As well as these provisions *all* the main human rights instruments contain articles outlining standards for a fair trial, and other standards relating to the due process of law that governments must follow when an individual accused of a crime is prosecuted.

When a government lives up to these standards in imposing a death sentence, the execution is not extrajudicial. However, in some cases governments have formally imposed the death penalty but failed to comply with the procedural safeguards prescribed in international law. In such cases, the government has clearly violated international law, and has illegally and arbitrarily deprived a person of his or her life.

Whether such cases constitute extrajudicial executions, however, is more difficult to decide. The spectrum ranges from cases with only a single procedural defect to those with such pervasively defective procedures that the accused can be said to have had a trial in name only. There are strong arguments for excluding all such cases from the category of extrajudicial executions. The existence of judicial procedures must be recognized as positive, no matter how defective they may be. International legal standards exist against which the procedures may be judged and pressure can be exerted on a government if it fails to live up to those standards. Institutional structures for dealing with such cases in the country may improve as a result. If, on the other hand, rudimentary or inadequate procedures are dismissed and the resultant executions included in a broad category with government killings where no procedures have been followed, the opportunity to build on and improve existing procedural structures has been lost.

Killings in connection with law enforcement

Another category of killings which, at least in some cases, is acceptable under international law is that of killings committed in connection with enforcement of the law. It is implicit in the international human rights instruments that the rights they guarantee, including an individual's right to life, must be balanced against respect for the rights and freedoms of others. When this balance is correctly applied, any resulting deprivation of an individual's rights, including if necessary the right to life, is not arbitrary or illegal.

The Code of Conduct for Law Enforcement Officials was adopted by the UN General Assembly in 1979. In Article 3 it states that "(l)aw enforcement officials may use force only when strictly necessary and to the extent required for the performance of their duty". The commentary to Article 3, which the UN committee drawing up the code called "an integral part of the code", specifies that "(i)n no case should this provision be interpreted to authorize the use of force which is disproportionate to the legitimate objective to be achieved". The commentary states that "(i)n general, firearms should not be used except when a suspected offender offers armed resistance or otherwise jeopardizes the lives of others and less extreme measures are not sufficient to restrain or apprehend the suspected offender".

This general approach is far more restrictive than that of the European Convention. Article 2(2) uses the following formulation:

"Deprivation of life shall not be regarded as inflicted in contravention of this article when it results from the use of force which is no more than absolutely necessary:

(a) in defence of any person from unlawful violence;

(b) in order to effect a lawful arrest or to prevent the escape of a person lawfully detained;

(c) in action lawfully taken for the purpose of quelling a riot or insurrection."

This seems to authorize the use of any degree of force necessary to achieve "legitimate" ends. The fact that these are very broadly defined constitutes a weakness. To take its objects in turn:

(a) *Defence from unlawful violence*: It is a proper function of the authorities to protect citizens from unlawful violence. But it is easy to imagine situations in which this violence could be less than might justify the use of lethal force to suppress it.

(b) *To effect arrest or prevent escape*: These are normal law-enforcement tasks; however, considering the number of offences for which people can be arrested and how little evidence against a suspect is needed to justify an arrest, it is disturbing that the convention seems to legitimate the use of lethal force in order to arrest or detain any suspected offender.

(c) *To quell a riot or insurrection*: It is disquieting that the terms "riot" and "insurrection" are given the same weight. Riots are not necessarily directed against people: indeed, they are often against property. To suggest that the use of lethal force, if it is necessary to quell the latter kind of riot, is legitimate, raises serious questions.

The other basic human rights instruments do not deal specifically with this category of killing.

The draft Body of Principles for the Protection of All Persons under Any Form of Detention or Imprisonment is being considered by the UN General Assembly at the committee level in 1982. Although it does not address directly the question of when a prison officer might be justified in using force against a prisoner (other than to prohibit outright in Principle 5 the use of "torture or other cruel, inhuman or degrading treatment or punishment"), it does provide in Principle 30 a remedy for the use of unjustified force leading to death:

> "Whenever the death or disappearance of a detained or
> imprisoned person occurs during or shortly after the
> termination of his detention or imprisonment, an inquiry into
> the cause of death or disappearance shall be held by a
> judicial or other authority, either of its own motion or at the
> instance of a member of the family of such a person or any
> citizen who has a reliable knowledge of the case."

In addition, Principle 31 provides that the dependent members
of the family of an unjustly killed prisoner should have an
enforceable right to compensation for damages suffered as a result
of such a killing.

This question–when is a killing justified in connection with law
enforcement–has to some extent been covered by existing and
currently evolving international legal standards. The treatment
accorded this problem in international law has, however, been less
than comprehensive. Yet this is an area of vital importance in
confronting the issue of extrajudicial executions.

Killings in war

The International Covenant (Article 4), the American Convention
(Article 27) and the European Convention (Article 15) specifically
state that the protection of the right to life remains in force in
times of war or other public emergency.

In addition, a number of international legal standards have been
articulated dealing specifically with killings in time of war and
other armed conflicts. These standards are meant to delineate
acceptable standards of behaviour for participants in such conflicts.

Such standards were first formally enunciated after the Second
World War in the 1945 Charter of the International Military
Tribunal (the "Nuremberg Charter"), under which the Nuremberg
Tribunal was set up. The Nuremberg Charter specified three
categories of "crimes under international law": crimes against
peace, war crimes and crimes against humanity. It defined crimes
against humanity to include "murder, extermination, enslavement, deportation and other inhumane acts committed against any
civilian population, before or during the war, or persecutions on
political, racial or religious grounds in execution of or in connection with any crime within the jurisdiction of the Tribunal,
whether or not in violation of the domestic law of the country
where perpetrated". The General Assembly, in a resolution

adopted in 1946,[1] affirmed the international legal principles recognized by the Nuremberg Charter, specifying however that the definition of "crimes against humanity" applied only to acts which were war-related.

Certain consequences under international law flow from the designation of these particular acts as crimes against humanity. No statutory limitation is applicable, meaning that no time limit exists within which those accused of such crimes may be prosecuted.[2] Those who have committed crimes against humanity cannot claim asylum or refugee status.[3] Finally, accused individuals may be subject to universal jurisdiction, that is, they can be prosecuted wherever they may be.

The Geneva Conventions of 12 August 1949 on the Protection of Victims of War are also relevant. Each of the four conventions deal with a particular group of "protected persons": the wounded and sick in armed forces in the field (Convention I); the wounded, sick and shipwrecked members of armed forces at sea (Convention II); prisoners of war (Convention III); and civilians in time of war (Convention IV). These four conventions (as supplemented by Additional Protocols I and II in 1977) prescribe as minimum standards a full panoply of procedural safeguards which must be adhered to in death penalty cases in times of war or armed conflict, including specific provisions for armed conflicts which are not international.

Each of the Geneva Conventions clearly prohibits murder and other acts of violence against protected persons. They explicitly provide that "wilful killings" are to be considered "grave breaches" of the Geneva Conventions, that is, war crimes subject to universality of jurisdiction. Similarly, Article 75 of Additional Protocol I prohibits "violence to ... life ... in particular ... murder" against *all* people (whether or not they are protected persons) who are in the power of one of the sides in an international armed conflict. The Geneva Conventions also prohibit "at any time and in any place whatsoever ... violence to life and person, in particular, murder of all kinds", in armed conflict which is not international in character (Article 3 in each).

Article 4 of Additional Protocol II covers people who are not taking a direct part, or have ceased to take part, in hostilities

[1] Resolution 95 (I), 11 December 1946

[2] Pursuant to the Convention on the Non-Applicability of Statutory Limitations to War Crimes and Crimes against Humanity.

[3] The UN Declaration on Territorial Asylum and the Convention and Protocol Relating to the Status of Refugees exclude such claims.

during an armed conflict which is not international: it prohibits violence to life "at any time and in any place whatsoever".

The international legal standards applicable to killings in war are relatively extensive and well-developed. The International Committee of the Red Cross and other organizations have consistently worked for the development and implementation of such standards.

Genocide and other crimes under international law; torture; 'disappearances'

Under the Nuremberg Charter a variety of war-related crimes including murder were designated "crimes under international law" and the prosecution of alleged offenders was made subject to particular rules. Since the signing of the Nuremberg Charter there has been some attempt to extend the category of "crimes under international law" to include acts not related to war. The most successful move in this direction relates to the crime of genocide.

In 1946 the UN General Assembly passed a resolution affirming that genocide–defined as denial of the right to existence of entire human groups–was a crime under international law.[4] It called upon member states to enact necessary domestic legislation and to initiate appropriate international cooperation to prevent and punish the crime. It also requested the UN Economic and Social Council (ECOSOC) to prepare a draft convention on the subject for submission to the next session of the General Assembly.

The resulting Convention on the Prevention and Punishment of the Crime of Genocide was presented to the UN General Assembly in 1948. The genocide convention, in Article II, defines as "genocide" a number of acts, including killings, "committed with intent to destroy, in whole or in part, a national, ethnical, racial or religious group" whether in peacetime or during a war. It states, in Article IV, that those committing such acts "shall be punished, whether they are constitutionally responsible rulers, public officials or private individuals". The definition of genocide was highly controversial, particularly the omission of "political groups" as potential victims of genocide.

A major procedural weakness of the genocide convention relates to genocidal acts committed with the connivance of the state. The genocide convention provides that prosecutions are to be by a competent tribunal in the state itself or "by such

[4] Resolution 96 (I), 11 December 1946

international penal tribunal as may have jurisdiction with respect to those Contracting Parties which shall have accepted its jurisdiction". An offending state is hardly likely to agree to either of these alternatives. Article IX does include an arbitration clause under which disputes between states relating to the interpretation, application or fulfilment of the genocide convention can be submitted to the International Court of Justice, but many states have made reservations regarding the court's jurisdiction in such cases.

Further attempts to extend the category of "crimes under international law" not related to war have not been successful. When the UN General Assembly in 1946 affirmed the principles of the Nuremberg Charter by Resolution 95 (I), it also instructed the Committee on the Codification of International Law (subsequently, the International Law Commission, a UN expert body responsible for the development of international law) to formulate a general codification of the offences against the peace and security of mankind. This was undertaken by the International Law Commission in 1950. A draft Code of Offences against the Peace and Security of Mankind was produced in 1951, commented upon by governments, and a revised version released in 1954. The offences listed in the draft code are not necessarily war-related and include, in Article 2(11), "(i)nhuman acts such as murder, extermination, enslavement, deportation or persecutions, committed against any civilian population on social, political, racial, religious or cultural grounds by the authorities of a State or by private individuals acting at the instigation or with the toleration of such authorities". Extrajudicial executions are clearly covered. The UN General Assembly, however, never adopted the code. On 10 December 1981 the 36th Session of the General Assembly adopted Resolution 36/106 inviting the International Law Commission to resume its work on the draft code. The difficult jurisdictional and enforcement problems which arise with respect to "crimes under international law" make many governments wary of pursuing an enlargement of this category of offence.

Neither torture nor "disappearances" are mentioned in the draft code although it has been suggested that such human rights violations should be included. Other initiatives against torture and "disappearances", however, are relevant to extrajudicial executions because these violations are closely connected. The Declaration on the Protection of All Persons from Torture and Other Cruel, Inhuman or Degrading Treatment or Punishment (the "torture declaration"), adopted by the UN General Assembly in 1975, and the draft torture convention currently (in 1982) being considered condemn acts often associated with extrajudicial executions. Similarly, the UN General Assembly Resolution 33/173 in 1978 on people who have "disappeared" after being taken into custody, and the work of the UN Working Group on Enforced or Involuntary Disappearances, concern the fate of individuals who may in fact be the victims of extrajudicial executions. The initiatives taken to combat "disappearances" in particular show how the international community has reacted constructively to a very specific category of human rights violation.

Recent initiatives

The international community has only recently begun to define as a separate and unique category the various sorts of killings which are extrajudicial executions.

Resolution 5 on "extra-legal executions", passed by the Sixth United Nations Congress on the Prevention of Crime and the Treatment of Offenders ("Sixth UN Congress") in 1980, represents the most comprehensive effort in this area. The preamble cites the Universal Declaration of Human Rights and the International Covenant on the right to life, the four Geneva Conventions on the illegality of killing in armed conflict, the UN General Assembly resolution on the "disappeared" and the torture declaration, as well as referring to the illegality of murder under all national legal systems. The resolution "deplores and condemns" and affirms as "a particularly abhorrent crime":

"the practice of killing and executing political opponents or suspected offenders carried out by armed forces, law enforcement or other governmental agencies or by paramilitary or political groups acting with the tacit or other support of such forces or agencies".

This definition is less than precise. The reference to "suspected offenders", for example, is unclear. However, it is the best formulation framed by an intergovernmental body so far.

Subsequent initiatives have been less helpful. UN General Assembly Resolution 35/172 on "arbitrary or summary executions", adopted on 15 December 1980, expresses alarm "at the incidence in different parts of the world of summary executions as well as of arbitrary executions". The resolution, however, makes no attempt to define what sorts of killings are meant to be covered, and seems to be limiting its scope to cases where the death penalty has been *judicially* imposed without providing full procedural safeguards.

A resolution adopted in 1981 by the UN Sub-Commission on Prevention of Discrimination and Protection of Minorities[5] drew the attention of the UN Commission on Human Rights to the increasing scale of "politically-motivated executions"; again it offered no explanation of the types of killings to be encompassed. This resolution is, however, somewhat innovative in recommending that the Commission on Human Rights "request the Economic and Social Council to call upon Governments to abolish capital punishment for political offences".

The UN General Assembly's most recent resolution on "arbitrary or summary executions" was adopted on 9 November 1981.[6] While the language is somewhat stronger than that of the 1980 resolution, it still lacks clarity in its definitions. This resolution, *inter alia*,

"1. *Condemns* the practice of summary executions and arbitrary executions;
2. *Strongly deplores* the increasing number of summary executions as well as the continued incidence of arbitrary executions in different parts of the world; (and)
3. *Notes with concern* the occurrence of executions which are widely regarded as being politically motivated ...".

"Summary executions", "arbitrary executions" and "executions which are widely regarded as being politically motivated" remain somewhat elusive concepts.

The UN Commission on Human Rights, in its Resolution 1982/29 adopted in March 1982 and subsequently confirmed by the UN Economic and Social Council, makes clear that it considers "extra-legal executions" to fall within the definition of "summary or arbitrary executions". Noting that it is "(*d*)*eeply alarmed* about the occurrence of summary or arbitrary executions, including extra-legal executions, that are widely regarded as being politically motivated", it calls for the appointment for one year of "a special rapporteur to examine the questions related to summary or arbitrary executions".

Remedies

Although international law has not yet provided a careful definition of extrajudicial executions there already exists a broad range of international legal standards applicable to extrajudicial executions in their various forms.

[5] UN Doc E/C.N. 4/Sub. 2/1.769
[6] Resolution 36/22, 9 November 1981

The intergovernmental machinery for implementing these standards remains inadequate, however. Intergovernmental organizations have in recent years created significantly improved institutions to respond to gross violations of human rights, but consideration of extrajudicial executions within these institutions has often been on an *ad hoc* and sporadic basis. Their ability to enforce decisions remains limited. Institutions which may take action against extrajudicial executions include:

UN Commission on Human Rights. Under ECOSOC Resolution 1235 (XLII) the commission is authorized to undertake studies of situations of "gross violations" of human rights, the results of which are reported publicly. The situations in El Salvador, Guatemala and Bolivia have recently been scrutinized under this procedure.

Alternatively, under ECOSOC Resolution 1503 (XLVIII), the commission may review situations "which appear to reveal a consistent pattern of gross and reliably attested violations of human rights and fundamental freedoms". This procedure is lengthier and confidential.

UN Working Group on Enforced or Involuntary Disappearances. The working group, established by the commission in 1980, receives direct communications from institutions and individuals about specific cases of "disappearances". It has set up an emergency procedure to make direct and rapid contact with the governments concerned. Its ability to react swiftly on individual cases makes it particularly valuable. The mandate of the working group may extend to those extrajudicial executions which follow unacknowledged captivity by the authorities.

Human Rights Committee. Under the Optional Protocol to the International Covenant on Civil and Political Rights, individual complaints may be sent to the Human Rights Committee about violations of rights set forth in the Covenant, including the right to life. Article 41 of the Covenant permits one state party to the Covenant to complain about violations by another state party to it.

Regional organizations. Regional organizations such as the European Parliament and the Inter-American Commission on Human Rights have sent fact-finding missions to various parts of the world and published reports drawing regional and world attention to human rights abuses including extrajudicial executions.

UN Special Rapporteur on Summary or Arbitrary Executions. In March 1982 the UN Commission on Human Rights recommended the appointment of a special rapporteur to collect information and submit "a comprehensive report to the Commission on

Human Rights at its thirty-ninth session [in February-March 1983] on the occurrence and extent of the practice of such [summary or arbitrary] executions together with his conclusions and recommendations . . .'' The exact role of the rapporteur has not yet been defined. However, in addition to recording historically and analyzing the circumstances surrounding such killings, the rapporteur might be in a position to bring killings currently taking place to the attention of the United Nations for immediate action.

Conclusion

The lack of a precise definition of extrajudicial executions is not an insurmountable problem. Although no single instrument exists which describes and condemns all the various killings which ought to be encompassed in such a concept, the range of existing international level instruments can be said to cover the field with some degree of comprehensiveness. Any approach to dealing effectively with extrajudicial executions should include the widest possible dissemination of information about these international legal standards; what is also needed is continued surveillance. to see that they are utilized and developed to their best potential.

The International Conference on Extrajudicial Executions

The International Conference on Extrajudicial Executions was held in Noordwijkerhout, the Netherlands, some 50 kilometres west of Amsterdam, from 30 April to 2 May 1982. Over 120 people from 30 countries took part. Some 60 experts attended in their personal capacity: members of intergovernmental and non-governmental organizations, human rights activists and academics. Another 60 participants were from Amnesty International bodies: the International Executive Committee, the International Secretariat and more than 20 sections.

The conference began with a public opening session. Dirk van Norren, Chairperson of Amnesty International's Dutch Section, stressed the importance of participants spreading the ideas discussed at the conference among members of their organizations. The Dutch Foreign Affairs Minister, Max van der Stoel, then spoke. Extrajudicial executions are one of the most horrible violations of human rights, he said. States which committed this violation could lawfully be called to account for their conduct. He outlined some of the ways in which the Dutch Government, particularly in cooperation with other governments, could help prevent such killings: by training and informing diplomats, who would report on local conditions; by development cooperation to relieve inequalities of wealth and power; by restrictive arms policies; by action in international bodies; by the dissemination of information; and by assistance in promoting independent judiciaries, in training lawyers and law enforcement officers, in improving fact-finding machinery and provisions and in creating human rights awareness programs.

The final speaker at the opening seminar was Thomas Hammarberg, Secretary General of Amnesty International. During the past decade hundreds of thousands of people in different countries had been victims of extrajudicial executions, he said. In some cases the full scale of killings was not known: there was an *information crisis*. It was important for the conference to find ways of rapid and reliable fact-finding and dissemination of reports and to secure the protection of those who gave information. In other

cases the facts were known but effective action could not be taken
— an *action crisis*. Accountability, he said, was key: soldiers and
police officers are accountable to their superiors, senior officers to
the political authorities and those in authority to the community at
large and the international community.

The rest of the conference was closed to the public. The plenary
session considered the concept of extrajudicial executions and its
terminology, and the scope of the conference. The conference
then divided into four working parties on:

–fact-finding and information
–non-governmental approaches
–intergovernmental organizations and legal standards
–the international context of extrajudicial executions

Two special meetings were held: on the armed forces and the
police as agents of extrajudicial executions; and on the role of
journalists. A number of experts from those professions were
invited to these meetings.

At the final plenary session reports from the four working
parties were presented and amended. A draft final statement was
presented and adopted by the conference with amendments from
the floor. The conference was followed by a public event in an
Amsterdam theatre, attended by nearly two thousand people.
Theo van Boven, former Director of the UN Division of Human
Rights, Piet Dankert, President of the European Parliament and
Roberto Cuellar of the *Socorro Jurídico* (legal aid office of the
Archbishopric) in El Salvador spoke of their personal experiences
of opposing political killings by governments. There was also
music and a performance by a theatre group.

Working party reports

Working Party A: fact-finding and information

Working Party A was charged with examining the problem of
investigating political killings by governments and of how the
information obtained could best be disseminated. The working
party heard a series of presentations on problems of investigation in
various countries. The following points emerged in the discussion:

Governments often try to cover up extrajudicial executions by
denying that killings have taken place, by attributing the killings to

opposition or insurgent forces, or by justifying them as the result of armed encounters with government forces or of attempts by the victims to escape. Governments may also undermine or destroy national institutions that could investigate and redress extrajudicial executions. They have impeded independent investigations in various ways:

—emasculating the judiciary through purges: doing away with security of tenure for judges; reducing the legal authority of the judiciary or transferring jurisdiction to military courts; or delaying or refusing requests for information by the judiciary;

—ending safeguards such as *habeas corpus*, the right to immediate access to counsel or immediate delivery to courts or judicial officers;

—threatening, assaulting or filing criminal charges against lawyers, witnesses and families of victims of extrajudicial executions;

—granting amnesties or immunity from criminal prosecution or civil suit to suspected perpetrators of extrajudicial executions;

—destroying the independence of the prosecuting authority;

—eliminating investigation by the legislature;

—creating special police or security forces which are not subject to normal supervision.

Sometimes governments go through the motions of investigating extrajudicial executions but the result is merely a cover-up. Sometimes they conduct investigations but fail to act on the results.

Minimum standards to establish that a government had investigated reports of extrajudicial executions in good faith could possibly be set down. Among such standards might be: an impartial judge; public hearings; participation at all stages of the investigation by the family of the victim and their lawyer; full access to military records of personnel that could identify the person(s) responsible; publication of findings; the right of appeal.

If, on the other hand, a government took actions threatening or destroying institutions capable of investigating extrajudicial executions, this could be taken as an indication that no investigations in good faith were being undertaken.

When political killings by governments are passed off as killings in "armed confrontations" or killings in "self-defence", a government is claiming that the killings took place in circumstances which could make them permissible under international standards. Such claims might be confronted by establishing that the victim was unarmed or in custody. At other times governments justify killings by claiming an overriding purpose of state such as "national security". Such claims do not require factual refutation; under international standards no state may derogate from the absolute right to protection from arbitrary deprivation of life.

Political killings by governments are difficult to investigate and it is usually impossible to obtain all the relevant details. Even where a country has not closed its doors to outside observers, investigation is hampered by limited access, by intimidation of witnesses and by official measures taken to cover up the crime.

A number of kinds of evidence must be taken into account in establishing whether an extrajudicial execution has occurred: confirmation of death; evidence that the victim was killed and that the killing was intentional; evidence of official responsibility, which might be established through eye-witness accounts or through reports from sources with direct access to the parties involved. A consistent pattern of killings of political opponents of a government without preventive action being taken by the government could often be a strong indication of government complicity in a killing which fitted that pattern. It would also be suggestive if normal procedures were not followed: if a death was not followed by an inquest or post-mortem examination or if normal reports of arrests or military operations were not submitted.

However, such indications do not necessarily prove that an extrajudicial execution has occurred – the existence of a pattern does not prove that a particular killing was an extrajudicial execution, nor does the absence of a pattern disprove an extrajudicial execution.

Certain governmental actions or institutional changes in a country could sometimes signal the existence of "preconditions" for political killings by governments and other human rights violations. Among such possible indicators are:

–the imposition of a state of emergency, martial law, or other states of exception;

–the occurrence of other human rights violations such as irregular arrests and detentions, "disappearances" and torture;

–the existence of secret places of detention;

–the identification of certain groups as "enemies";

–the creation of irregular or paramilitary groups for action against opposition movements;

–claims of "encounters" with armed groups resulting in deaths;

–claims of deaths resulting from escape attempts;

–the appearance of unmarked graves in cemeteries.

It was suggested that a list of such indicators could serve as an "alert system" or "early warning system" for possible extrajudicial executions and other human rights violations.

There are many possible sources of information on political killings by governments. Among them are domestic human rights groups; survivors, including eye-witnesses who were potential victims; relatives, including organized groups of relatives; lawyers; and written documentation arising from court actions. Journalists and diplomats could also sometimes furnish information on extrajudicial executions. Official government statements might contain information which confirms, partially substantiates, or is inconsistent with evidence gathered from other sources, but human rights groups must be aware of such government data so as to be able to respond.

Domestic human rights groups are crucial in monitoring and acting to prevent political killings by governments. The working party agreed that international human rights organizations should develop systematic ways of responding when domestic groups are threatened by their governments.

Working Party B: non-governmental approaches

Working Party B was charged with examining the role that non-governmental organizations should play in a campaign to stop extrajudicial executions. It also discussed the possible tone and content of such a campaign. In addition, the working party touched briefly on the role of non-governmental organizations in gathering and disseminating information.

A campaign to stop political killings by governments was the major item discussed by the working party. It recommended setting up a small committee, convened by Amnesty International, to coordinate the activities of various non-governmental organizations in such a campaign. The proposed committee would be made up of one individual representing each of the following groups: the churches, trade unions, the legal community, relatives of victims, and human rights organizations. The committee could explore the possibility of setting up an "urgent action network" of non-governmental organizations to come to the defence of local human rights activists endangered because of their work in gathering information on extrajudicial executions. Another proposal was to circulate a petition for signature by non-governmental organizations in favour of a UN General Assembly resolution condemning extrajudicial executions and recommending UN action. Coordination among non-governmental organizations should also be established at the national level, and liaison committees for that purpose were suggested.

The campaign itself should convey the scale of extrajudicial executions and the complicity of governments. It should emphasize that the victims of extrajudicial executions are at the mercy of their killers; they are not killed in circumstances of reciprocal violence. Victims often suffer horribly under torture before being executed. It should put a human face on the issue, by focusing on individual cases and presenting testimonies from relatives of victims. The campaign should stress the universal and basic "right to live".

The great potential of using artistic material to dramatize the problem, and to prevent campaigning from becoming mechanical, should be exploited. Up-to-date information should be compiled and publicized regularly. For example, a "log" of extrajudicial executions could be sent to governments, organizations and the news media.

Members of certain professions, such as lawyers, journalists and doctors, could be enlisted in efforts to halt political killings by governments. They bring special skills to bear on the issue, and are naturally concerned when members of their own profession are at risk. Members of these professions could be sent on fact-finding missions to countries where extrajudicial executions occur or are threatened.

The campaign should support groups of relatives of victims who raise public awareness through their personal testimonies and activities.

Those who arm or train the killers also bear responsibility for political killings by governments. Measures should be taken against international transfers of military, security and police weapons and training, where these are used in the commission of extrajudicial executions. Participants suggested that consideration should be given to the issue of economic aid to countries that carry out extrajudicial executions; this issue might be raised with banks, multinational corporations and international lending agencies.

Some local human rights organizations face difficulties in communicating information on extrajudicial executions to international organizations which could disseminate and act on it, for example, because of lack of funds. It was recommended that Amnesty International review the problem of communications with domestic and international human rights organizations and with victims of human rights violations. Consideration should also be given to ways in which governments could be encouraged to provide or make public information on human rights violations gathered by their embassies in the field.

Working Party C: intergovernmental bodies and legal standards

Working Party C was charged with considering the adequacy and relevance of existing international legal standards relating to extra-judicial executions, and with surveying the relevant mechanisms for action by intergovernmental organizations.

The working party discussed a number of international legal instruments and other standards now being developed. Political killings by governments are already clearly unlawful under existing international legal instruments and customary international law. Certain existing legal instruments could, however, be improved and further ones adopted. Four basic principles should be applied in the development of standards on extrajudicial executions: perpetrators should be subject to prosecution for their crimes, no matter what country they are in; there should be no time limit on prosecutions; generally no granting of asylum; and perpetrators should be liable to be tried before any international penal court which might be established.

The working party surveyed the various mechanisms for action by international and regional intergovernmental organizations: UN bodies, including the Working Group on Enforced or Involuntary Disappearances, the Working Group on Communications, the Human Rights Committee, the United Nations Educational, Scientific and Cultural Organization (UNESCO); the International Labour Organisation; the European Commission on Human Rights; and the African Commission on Human and Peoples' Rights to be established under the African Charter on Human and Peoples' Rights. Such mechanisms fit into three general categories: preventive, mitigating and remedial.

It is not enough to report on situations after the event. Urgent mechanisms must establish direct contact with governments and react quickly to emergency human rights situations. The possibility of the UN setting up an "early warning" system for situations of gross human rights violations was discussed; such a system would depend heavily on input from local UN representatives and non-governmental organizations. There was discussion of recent resolutions adopted by the UN Economic and Social Council relating to the Central African Republic, Equatorial Guinea and Uganda. These aimed to help the recovery of countries which had recently suffered serious human rights violations by providing assistance such as training programs for the police.

A number of general conclusions were drawn:

–Many intergovernmental mechanisms exist, and it is an effective strategy to use as many relevant mechanisms as possible in order to give maximum publicity to political killings by any government. International and regional mechanisms are both important and should complement each other.

–Interested individuals and organizations should be given the right to make complaints, including the family of the victim, potential victims, other interested parties, non-governmental organizations and, in the case of regional organizations, individuals and entities from outside the region.

–The independence of personnel on intergovernmental bodies dealing with such cases is of paramount importance.

–Such bodies should exchange information to enhance their mutual effectiveness. Government replies should be forwarded to complainants for response.

–On-the-spot visits and other direct contacts are extremely important.

–Such bodies and their chief officers should be willing to intercede directly and promptly whenever necessary.

Working Party D: the international context

Working Party D was charged with examining international aspects of extrajudicial executions. It also considered the national contexts in which killings occur.

Governments order or condone unlawful political killings for many different reasons. For example, political killings may be carried out to counteract killings by opposition forces where the existing judicial institutions are not considered strong enough to deal with them, or where an urgency is perceived which does not allow for lengthy judicial proceedings. They are used to deter opposition activities, to eliminate peaceful dissenters, to impede judicial proceedings through assassinations of judges and lawyers, or to facilitate forceful evictions from land. They are also used to entrench power after revolutionary change or to extend power to areas where central control is shaky. Sometimes they occur in the course of competition for power within a ruling group.

Although many governments face economic problems and political threats only some respond by resorting to political killings. A pattern of extrajudicial executions might characterize a state in extreme crisis, willing to resort to extreme measures of social control.

Reviewing political killings by governments in different countries, members of the working party said that centralized decisions about counter-insurgency practices or the deployment of armed forces were often implemented in a relatively decentralized way by local military commanders who carried out the killings. In some countries local landowners or provincial officials could carry out killings with the acquiescence of the government.

A government policy of unlawful killings had sometimes been introduced as a result of foreign military intervention in a country. In other cases extrajudicial executions had been fostered by international transfers of arms or military training. Restrictions on international trade in arms used to commit extrajudicial executions, although desirable, are difficult to effect because of the number of different suppliers.

The indoctrination of military personnel which often takes place in international training programs could give trainees a simplistic view of domestic unrest. Opponents of the government are often identified as servants of a foreign enemy, to be liquidated by whatever method. It was proposed that such indoctrination be counteracted by training military personnel in their responsibilities under international humanitarian law and other international standards.

Further study on a number of topics could assist in the elaboration of measures against political killings by governments. For example, the curricula of military academies around the world could be surveyed to see if they included doctrines legitimatizing extrajudicial executions and to estimate the possibility of increasing training in human rights issues.

Journalism, human rights and extrajudicial executions

The special meeting was attended by invited Dutch reporters and editors as well as regular conference participants. It dealt with the protection of journalists and with improving the quality of reporting on extrajudicial executions.

The special nature of journalism and its attendant dangers require recognition. Journalists themselves are often reticent about publicizing the tribulations of their work; clear danger, such as the publication of "death lists" naming journalists, often receives little publicity.

It was generally felt that the best protection is solidarity within the communications media and among journalists' organizations. Several speakers described the efforts of journalists' organizations in North America and Europe to protect colleagues abroad. There was some discussion of an internationally recognized press card, but the idea was rejected by most speakers because of the dangers of government control and infiltration.

Reporting of political killings by governments is frequently inaccurate. In one country where people are being killed by government forces every day the deaths are usually reported in the foreign press as "the right killing the left and the left killing the right". Various causes of poor reporting were mentioned: lack of initiative on the part of journalists; government pressure; editorial pressure; or, in many dangerous situations, lack of alternatives to officially provided information.

The meeting recommended a conference of journalists' organizations, other media professional organizations and human rights groups to discuss political killings by governments, the dangers for the journalists, and how to gain maximum publicity to stop this violation of human rights.

The armed forces and the police as agents of extrajudicial executions

The meeting was attended by specially invited Dutch military and police officers and specialists in military and police studies, as well as regular conference participants. It examined ways of influencing military and police personnel who carry out human rights violations in repressive countries. It also examined possible approaches to the military and police in non-repressive countries.

It is important to distinguish between military forces and the police, as well as between various forces and units within the two professions. Distinctions should be drawn between military forces primarily concerned with external security and those involved in internal security matters; between military forces playing a law enforcement role and those playing a conventional military role; and between regular police units involved in ordinary law

110

enforcement and special units, such as plainclothes or paramilitary units, concerned with security and intelligence.

International humanitarian law applies to the conduct of armed conflicts; it is normally the concern of the armed forces, not the police. On the other hand, international police organizations were involved in drawing up the Code of Conduct for Law Enforcement Officials but military components with similar functions, such as military police, were not consulted and consequently attached little importance to this code and did not feel that it concerned them. In principle, the code is applicable to all military units with a law enforcement role.

The International Committee of the Red Cross has a key role in educating armed forces throughout the world in humanitarian law. However there is also a great need to develop a more specific awareness of human rights issues among military personnel, particularly because of the law enforcement role played by military units in many countries. In this context development of special codes of conduct for military forces was discussed. Such codes, it was suggested, could play an important role in preventing military forces from committing human rights violations in times of political crisis.

It was suggested that members of human rights organizations could develop contacts with members of the armed forces by visiting military academies in their countries and encouraging human rights education within the armed forces. However the response to such approaches was unlikely to be positive unless a climate of concern for human rights already existed at the national level.

The meeting recommended studies to assess the characteristics of the armed forces in countries where repression is taking place. Such studies should encompass the armed forces' own perception of their role; their view of the world and interpretation of events in the country; the class, economic background, ethnic origins, race and political interests of officers; as well as the role, if any, played by the armed forces in law enforcement operations. Such studies could help in designing approaches to military forces in repressive countries.

As a follow-up to the conference, an international workshop should be organized orientated towards the military, and another orientated towards the police. The workshop for the military would be intended to facilitate the development of an international organization of military officers for the promotion of human rights and of a code or codes of conduct for the military profession. The workshop for the police would be intended to examine ways of encouraging the implementation of the Code of Conduct for Law Enforcement Officials.

Conclusions and recommendations

The following conclusions and recommendations were reached by members of the working parties. Some represent a consensus of views; others were the views of individual participants, or were suggestions which the working party felt should be given further consideration.

Fact-finding and information

Recognizing the need to strengthen the capacity of non-governmental organizations to investigate extrajudicial executions, Working Party A recommended that further consideration be given to the following ideas:

1. Minimum standards should be developed for investigations and the assessment of information by non-governmental organizations in cases of extrajudicial executions.

2. Minimum standards should be developed to establish that a government has investigated reports of extrajudicial executions in good faith.

3. Appropriate ways should be found to support local human rights organizations whose activities include the reporting of political killings by governments. In particular, links between local and international human rights organizations should be developed so that prompt and concerted action could be taken when domestic organizations were facing difficulties in carrying on their work.

4. Resources should be allocated to enable investigations to be pursued actively in the field and to ensure the rapid circulation of information gathered on investigative missions or resulting from the work of local non-governmental organizations.

5. Mechanisms should be developed to challenge the denial of access to observers by governments of countries where there are grounds to believe that extrajudicial executions are occurring.

6. Studies should be made of patterns of extrajudicial executions and of the concomitant social, economic, political and legal developments, with a view to establishing whether prompt, and, if possible, preventive action could be taken.

Non-governmental approaches

7. A public campaign to stop political killings by governments should stress the universal and basic "right to live". For the campaign to win support, it must infuse people with a sense of hope and achievement and not simply rely on a catalogue of horrors. Political killings by governments must therefore be shown to be preventable, and successful actions should be widely publicized. Attention should be given to devising means for preventing political killings by governments and not merely reacting after they have taken place.

8. Such a campaign should seek to convey the magnitude of extrajudicial executions as a worldwide problem and the complicity of governments.

9. The means of campaigning in the field of the arts should be explored – the possibility of arousing public opinion by means of literature, theatre and music. Bibliographies of films and other appropriate resources should be compiled.

10. Human rights organizations should coordinate their activities against extrajudicial executions in order to achieve maximum pressure, publicity and public support. In particular, it was recommended that a small committee be convened to coordinate the activities of various non-governmental organizations in a worldwide campaign to stop political killings by governments.

11. The possibility of bringing civil and penal suits against perpetrators of extrajudicial executions should be explored.

12. Efforts should be made to improve the accuracy of news reporting on political killings by governments. The news media should be encouraged to undertake investigative reporting about political killings.

Intergovernmental organizations and legal standards

13. Extrajudicial executions are crimes under national and international law for which states, as well as individuals acting as their agents, are responsible. Legal responsibility for such killings cannot be diminished under any circumstances including war or other public emergency threatening the life of the nation.

14. Accordingly, states are obliged not to commit, allow or condone extrajudicial executions and to take all necessary

legislative, executive and judicial measures to ensure that individual perpetrators are brought to justice.

15. States should prohibit and prevent any lethal use of force by law enforcement officials except where essential to protect life. States should also promote the formulation of and adherence to professional codes of conduct by members of the military and the police.

16. The responsibility to bring individual perpetrators of extra-judicial executions to justice before the proper forum is both national and international. To this end,

   (a) alleged perpetrators of extrajudicial executions should be held subject to universality of jurisdiction, which means that any state on whose territory they are found should ensure that they are brought to justice;

   (b) there should be no time limit for the adjudication of the crimes;

   (c) asylum should not be extended to perpetrators of extra-judicial executions*; and

   (d) perpetrators of extrajudicial executions should be sub-ject to any international penal court that may be estab-lished to adjudicate such crimes.

17. Without prejudice to the validity of the obligations under customary international law, all states should be urged to ratify the Convention on the Prevention and Punishment of the Crime of Genocide, the two Protocols additional to the Geneva Conventions of 12 August 1949, the International Covenant on Civil and Political Rights (including the Optional Protocol thereto) and the relevant regional human rights conventions, and to make the necessary declarations to permit individual and interstate complaints as well as access to the relevant judicial forums.

18. It is important that those mechanisms already existing on the international level be able to respond rapidly and effectively where there is evidence to suggest that extrajudicial execu-tions might be or are being committed.

19. Chief officers of intergovernmental organizations are urged to make prompt, full and imaginative use of their good offices in order to prevent or stop extrajudicial executions. The use of good offices should include, when appropriate, direct contacts with the authorities in the country involved.

* However, Amnesty International opposes anyone being forcibly sent from one country to another where they can reasonably expect to become a prisoner of conscience, or be subjected to torture or extrajudicial or judicial execution.

20. Governments are urged to take all measures available to them to prevent extrajudicial executions in other countries as well as their own, including diplomatic intercession, approaches to intergovernmental bodies, resort to public denunciation and appropriate sanctions.

21. Non-governmental organizations are urged to bring any relevant information on extrajudicial executions at their disposal to the attention of intergovernmental bodies and give such information maximum public dissemination.

International context

22. Procedures should be established for calling on embassies abroad to intervene immediately on behalf of people under imminent threat of extrajudicial execution.

23. Multi-national political parties should use their affiliation and contacts to restrain political killings by governments. Members of parliament should monitor and seek to prevent extrajudicial executions through such means as investigative missions and special reporting or hearings.

24. Consideration should be given to the diplomatic, economic and political isolation of governments engaging in widespread extrajudicial executions. Diplomatic sanctions might be invoked against governments refusing to allow international investigation into reports of extrajudicial executions in their countries.

25. Pressure should be put on supplier countries, including the passage of appropriate legislation, to stop international transfers of arms used in carrying out extrajudicial executions. To this end an international register could be created of transfers of arms used in extrajudicial executions.

26. Military and police personnel should be trained in the relevant principles of humanitarian law and other international standards forbidding extrajudicial executions.

27. Seminars, workshops and other meetings should be organized with military and police personnel to discuss extrajudicial executions and other human rights issues in relation to their respective professions.

28. Studies should be made of the ways in which counter-insurgency and military training programs may foster extrajudicial executions.

29. Studies should be made of the effects of doctrines such as "national security" in subordinating human rights to the supposed interests of the state.

List of Participants

The International Conference on Extrajudicial Executions was the result of a project begun by Amnesty International's Dutch Section in 1980. The conference was attended by members of Amnesty International's International Secretariat and the following participants:

Name	Country/Nationality
Abugattas, Juan	Peru
Ade-Banjo, B.A.	Nigeria
Backer, Dam	Netherlands
Baehr, Peter	Netherlands
Bat, Carole	France
Berberat, Marc-Alain	Switzerland
Berman, Maureen	USA
Bicudo, Helio Pereira	Brazil
Boven, Theo van	Switzerland
Braun, Ko	Netherlands
Bronkhorst, Daan	Netherlands
Burgers, Herman	Netherlands
Charny, Israel	Israel
Clark, Ramsey	USA
Coad, Malcolm	UK
Crook, Frances	UK
Cuellar, Roberto	El Salvador
Derian, Patricia	USA
Diokno, José	Philippines
Dollé, Sally	France
Dupuy, Pierre-Marie	France
Egeland, Jan	Norway
Eide, Asbjørn	Norway
Ennals, Martin	UK
Fernando, Desmond	Sri Lanka
Fischer, Anette	Denmark
Gaspar, Jorge	Venezuela
Ghimire, Shanker	Nepal
Grant, Stephanie	UK

Groen, Jaap	Netherlands
Grossman, Claudio	Chile
Hawk, David	USA
Heijder, Alfred	Netherlands
Herrmann, Dick	Netherlands
D'Hondt, Ludo	Belgium
Horowitz, Irving	USA
Hsu, Victor	Mauritius
Hummel, Harry	Netherlands
Johannessen, Finn E.	Norway
Kadefors, Roland	Sweden
Kamper, Teunis	Netherlands
Kaufman, Edy	Israel
Kemps, Adri	Netherlands
Konaris, Demosthenes	Greece
Kuper, Leo	USA
Kuster, Margriet	Netherlands
Letelier, Isabel	Chile
Levin, Leah	UK
Lindblom, Bo	Sweden
Lüthke, Karsten	FRG
MacDermot, Niall	Switzerland
Méndez, Juan	Argentina
Morris, Fred	Costa Rica
Nauta, Heleen	Netherlands
Norren, Dirk van	Netherlands
Offenberg, Willem	Netherlands
Omond, Roger	UK
Oosting, Dick	Netherlands
Opsahl, Torkel	Norway
Overath, Dieter	FRG
Pedersen, Preben Meier	Denmark
Pettiti, Louis-Edmond	France
Plant, Roger	UK
Posner, Michael	USA
Ramcharan, B.G.	France
Rosa, Karen	USA
Rotter, Frederike	Canada
Samson, Klaus	Switzerland
Scherrer, Nicky	Switzerland
Schneider, Franz	Austria
Sciuto, Franca	Italy
Shapiro-Libai, Nitza	Israel
Shawcross, William	UK
Sheleff, Leon	Israel
Smeeman, Garret	Ireland

Soysal, Mumtaz	Turkey
Stanojevic, Stanislav	France
Stearman, Kaye	UK
Tan, Lek Hor	UK
Terhal, Pieter	Netherlands
Thoolen, Hans	Switzerland
Tromp, Hylke	Netherlands
Vaart, Johanna van der	Netherlands
Vargas Carreño, Edmundo	USA
Vautier, Danielle	France
Viccica, Antoinette	Austria
Viera-Gallo, Antonio	Italy
Wako, Amos	Kenya
Weiss-Fagen, Patricia	USA
Williams, Althea	Belgium
Wipfler, William	USA
Wiseberg, Laurie	USA
Wolff, Michel	Belgium
Zalaquett, José	Chile

Conference officers

Chairpersons: Peter Baehr and José Zalaquett
Rapporteur: Johanna van der Vaart
Secretary: Daan Bronkhorst

Working Party A:
Chairperson: Michael Posner
Rapporteur: Victor Hsu

Working Party B:
Chairperson: Martin Ennals
Rapporteur: Laurie Wiseberg
Secretary: Frances Crook

Working Party C:
Chairperson: Pierre Dupuy
Rapporteur: Desmond Fernando

Working Party D:
Chairperson: Asbjørn Eide
Rapporteur: David Hawk

Special meeting on military and police:
Chairperson: Niall MacDermot

Special meeting on journalists:
Chairperson: Malcolm Coad
Secretary: Daan Bronkhorst

APPENDIX I

Resolution 5 adopted by the Sixth United Nations Congress on the Prevention of Crime and the Treatment of Offenders (on 1 September 1982)

Alarmed by reports of widespread killings of political opponents or suspected offenders carried out by armed forces, law enforcement or other governmental agencies or by paramilitary or political groups often acting with the tacit or other support of such forces or agencies.

Recalling that Article 3 of the Universal Declaration of Human Rights guarantees to everyone the right to life, liberty and security of person,

Recalling Article 6, Paragraph 1, of the International Covenant on Civil and Political Rights, according to which no one shall be arbitrarily deprived of his life,

Recalling that the four Geneva Conventions,[1] of 12 August 1949, provide that wilful killings are grave breaches of the conventions and that Article 3, common to the four conventions, in respect of non-international armed conflict, further prohibits at any time and in any place whatsoever violence to life and person, in particular murder of all kinds,

Considering that murder committed or tolerated by Governments is condemned by all national legal systems and, thus, by general principles of law,

Recalling General Assembly resolution 33/173 of 20 December 1978 on Disappeared Persons, and the fact that the enforced or involuntary disappearances referred to in that resolution are frequently related to murder committed or tolerated by Governments,

Considering that the above-mentioned acts also violate the Declaration on the Protection of All Persons from Being Subjected to Torture or Other Cruel, Inhuman or Degrading Treatment or Punishment, contained in General Assembly Resolution 3452 (XXX) of 9 December 1975,

    1.   *Deplores and condemns* the practice of killing of political opponents or of suspected offenders carried out by armed forces, law enforcement or other governmental agencies or by paramilitary or political groups acting with the tacit or other support of such forces or agencies;

1 United Nations, *Treaty Series*, vol. 75.

2. *Affirms* that such killings constitute a particularly abhorrent crime the eradication of which is a high international priority;

3. *Calls upon* all Governments to take effective measures to prevent such acts;

4. *Urges* all organs of the United Nations dealing with questions of crime prevention and of human rights to take all possible action to bring such acts to an end.

Final Statement of the
International Conference on Extrajudicial
Executions
Amsterdam, 2 May 1982

The International Conference on Extrajudicial Executions, convened in the Netherlands by Amnesty International from 30 April to 2 May 1982,

- **BELIEVING DEEPLY** that the arbitrary deprivation of human life is utterly indefensible in any circumstances and that governments have primary responsibility for ensuring the observance of this principle,
- **ANGERED** that governments engage in arbitrary killings of persons because of their political beliefs or activities, religion or ethnic origin,
- **DEMANDS** that governments stop these practices,
- **DECLARES** that the international community should regard extrajudicial executions as a matter of the gravest and most urgent concern and should make every effort to bring to an end this denial of the right to life.

Hundreds of thousands of people in the past 10 years have been victims of extrajudicial executions—unlawful and deliberate killings carried out by order of a government or with its complicity.

These killings continue day after day outside any judicial process and in denial of the protection of law.

These killings are carried out both by regular military and police forces and by special units created to function without normal supervision, by death squads operating with government complicity, and assassins acting against victims in other countries.

A pattern of extrajudicial executions is often accompanied by the suspension of constitutional rights, a weakening of the independence of the judiciary, intimidation of witnesses, suppression of evidence and failure to act upon the results of independent investigations.

Governments often seek to cover up extrajudicial executions. They deny that killings have taken place, they attribute them to opposition forces, or they try to pass them off as the result of armed encounters with government forces or of attempts by the victims to escape.

Many of the victims are subjected to "disappearance", illegal detention or torture before being killed.

The scope of killings ranges from assassinations to the wholesale liquidation of political opposition. The scale of the crime is sometimes not known to the international community before it has reached proportions that will damage a whole society for generations to come.

The principle of protection against arbitrary deprivation of life constitutes a value of paramount importance. This principle cannot be abandoned under any circumstances, however grave.

Extrajudicial executions are crimes for which governments and their agents are responsible under national and international law. Their accountability is not diminished by the commission of similar abhorrent acts by opposition groups or others, or by considerations of national security.

It is the duty of governments not to commit or condone extrajudicial executions, and to take all legislative, executive and judicial measures necessary to ensure that those directly or indirectly responsible for such acts are brought to justice, and that the families of victims are compensated for their moral and material sufferings. Alleged perpetrators should be submitted to universal jurisdiction—trial or extradition wherever they may be.

Recommendations

Extrajudicial executions can only be prevented through firmly rooted institutions in all countries capable of dealing with abuse of human rights of every kind. The conference recommendations in the following summary all have this aim.

• **Individuals should raise their voices to make governments stop these killings and to show support for those left behind. Human rights organizations should provide them the opportunity by disseminating relevant information as promptly and objectively as possible. Joint programs of action should be initiated exposing the involvement of governments in the killings and their responsibility to bring the practice to an immediate end. Particular attention should be given to preventive measures designed to protect individuals who are in immediate danger.**

• **Educational institutions should be encouraged to place greater stress on the principle that extrajudicial executions are not justifiable under any circumstances.**

• **Minimum standards should be developed to establish that a** government has investigated reports of extrajudicial executions in good faith.

• Military and police forces should ensure that their members are trained to uphold standards forbidding extrajudicial executions.

• Governments should take steps to ensure that extrajudicial executions are not fostered through military, security or police transfers and international training.

• Governments should permit independent investigation on their territories, press for such investigations elsewhere, and use their diplomatic channels for fact-finding and pressure.

• Intergovernmental bodies should use existing mechanisms for investigation, reporting, and good offices and other forms of speedy intervention.

The final statement of the International Conference on Extrajudicial Executions was endorsed by Amnesty International in June 1982 as a statement of concern and a platform for action by individuals, organizations and governments.

Amnesty International — a worldwide campaign

In recent years, people throughout the world have become more and more aware of the urgent need to protect human rights effectively in every part of the world.

- Countless men and women are in prison for their beliefs. They are being held as prisoners of conscience in scores of countries—in crowded jails, in labour camps and in remote prisons.
- Thousands of political prisoners are being held under administrative detention orders and denied any possibility of a trial or an appeal.
- Others are forcibly confined in psychiatric hospitals or secret detention camps.
- Many are forced to endure relentless, systematic torture.
- More than a hundred countries retain the death penalty.
- Political leaders and ordinary citizens are becoming the victims of abductions, "disappearances" and killings, carried out both by government forces and opposition groups.

An international effort

To end secret arrests, torture and killing requires organized and worldwide effort. Amnesty International is part of that effort.

Launched as an independent organization over 20 years ago, Amnesty International is open to anyone prepared to work universally for the release of prisoners of conscience, for fair trials for political prisoners and for an end to torture and executions.

The movement now has members and supporters in more than 150 countries. It is independent of any government, political group, ideology, economic interest or religious creed.

It began with a newspaper article, "The Forgotten Prisoners", published on 28 May 1961 in *The Observer* (London) and reported in *Le Monde* (Paris).

Announcing an impartial campaign to help victims of political persecution, the British lawyer Peter Benenson wrote:

124

> *Open your newspaper any day of the week and you will find a report from somewhere in the world of someone being imprisoned, tortured or executed because his opinions or religion are unacceptable to his government. . . . The newspaper reader feels a sickening sense of impotence. Yet if these feelings of disgust all over the world could be united into common action, something effective could be done.*

Within a week he had received more than a thousand offers of support—to collect information, publicize it and approach governments. The groundwork was laid for a permanent human rights organization that eventually became known as Amnesty International. The first chairperson of its International Executive Committee (from 1963 to 1974) was Sean MacBride, who received the Nobel Peace Prize in 1974 and the Lenin Prize in 1975.

The mandate

Amnesty International is playing a specific role in the international protection of human rights.

It seeks the *release* of men and women detained anywhere because of their beliefs, colour, sex, ethnic origin, language or religious creed, provided they have not used or advocated violence. These are termed *prisoners of conscience.*

It works for *fair and prompt trials* for *all political prisoners* and works on behalf of such people detained without charge or trial.

It opposes the *death penalty* and *torture* or other cruel, inhuman or degrading treatment or punishment of *all prisoners* without reservation.

This mandate is based on the civil and political rights set down in the United Nations Universal Declaration of Human Rights and it reflects the belief that these rights transcend the boundaries of nation, race and belief.

Through its practical work for prisoners, Amnesty International participates in the wider promotion and protection of civil, political, economic, social and cultural rights.

Amnesty International does not oppose or support any government or political system. Its members around the world include supporters of differing systems who agree on the defence of all people in all countries against imprisonment for their beliefs, and against torture and execution.

Amnesty International at work

The working methods of Amnesty International are based on the principle of international responsibility for the protection of human rights. The movement tries to take action wherever and whenever there are violations of those human rights falling within its mandate. Since it was founded, Amnesty International groups have intervened on behalf of more than 20,000 prisoners in over a hundred countries with widely differing ideologies.

A unique aspect of the work of Amnesty International groups— placing the emphasis on the need for *international* human rights work—is the fact that each group works on behalf of prisoners held in countries other than its own. At least two prisoner cases are assigned to each group; the cases are balanced geographically and politically to ensure impartiality.

There are now over 2,500 local Amnesty International groups throughout the world. There are sections in 41 countries (in Africa, Asia, the Americas, Europe and the Middle East) and individual members, subscribers and supporters in more than 100 other countries. Members do not work on cases in their own countries. No section, group or member is expected to provide information on their own country and no section, group or member has any responsibility for action taken or statements issued by the international organization concerning their own country.

Continuous research

The movement attaches the highest importance to balanced and accurate reporting of facts. All its activities depend on meticulous research into allegations of human rights violations. The International Secretariat in London (with a staff of 150, comprising nearly 30 nationalities) has a Research Department which collects and analyses information from a wide variety of sources. These include hundreds of newspapers and journals, government bulletins, transcriptions of radio broadcasts, reports from lawyers and humanitarian organizations, as well as letters from prisoners and their families. Amnesty International also sends fact-finding missions for on-the-spot investigations and to observe trials, meet prisoners and interview government officials. Amnesty International takes full responsibility for its published reports and if proved wrong on any point is prepared to issue a correction.

Once the relevant facts are established, information is sent to sections and groups for action. The members then start the work of trying to protect the individuals whose human rights are reported to have been violated. They send letters to government ministers and embassies. They organize public meetings, arrange special publicity events, such as vigils at appropriate government offices or embassies, and try to interest newspapers in the cases they have taken up. They ask their friends and colleagues to help in the effort. They collect signatures for international petitions and raise money to send relief, such as medicine, food and clothing, to the prisoners and their families.

A permanent campaign

In addition to case work on behalf of individual prisoners, Amnesty International members campaign for the abolition of torture and the death penalty. This includes trying to prevent torture and executions when people have been taken to known torture centres or sentenced to death. Volunteers in dozens of countries can be alerted in such cases, and within hours hundreds of telegrams and other appeals can be on their way to the government, prison or detention centre.

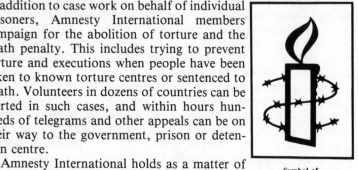

Symbol of
Amnesty International

Amnesty International holds as a matter of principle that the torture and execution of prisoners by *anyone*, including opposition groups, can never be accepted. Governments have the responsibility of dealing with such abuses, acting in conformity with international standards for the protection of human rights.

In its efforts to mobilize world public opinion, Amnesty International neither supports nor opposes economic or cultural boycotts. It *does* take a stand against the international transfer of military, police or security equipment and expertise likely to be used by recipient governments to detain prisoners of conscience and to inflict torture and carry out executions.

Amnesty International does not grade governments or countries according to their record on human rights. Not only does repression in various countries prevent the free flow of information about human rights abuses, but the techniques of repression and their impact vary widely. Instead of attempting comparisons, Amnesty International concentrates on trying to end the specific violations of human rights in each case.

Policy and funds

Amnesty International is a democratically run movement. Each year major policy decisions are taken by an International Council comprising representatives from all the sections. They elect an

International Executive Committee to carry out their decisions and supervise the day-to-day running of the International Secretariat.

The organization is financed by its members throughout the world, by individual subscriptions and donations. Members pay fees and conduct fund-raising campaigns—they organize concerts and art auctions and are often to be seen on fund-raising drives at street corners in their neighbourhoods.

Its rules about accepting donations are strict and ensure that any funds received by any part of the organization do not compromise it in any way, affect its integrity, make it dependent on any donor, or limit its freedom of activity.

The organization's accounts are audited annually and are published with its annual report.

Amnesty International has formal relations with the United Nations (ECOSOC), UNESCO, the Council of Europe, the Organization of African Unity and the Organization of American States.

INDEX

130

Makwana, Yogendra, 63
Mano Blanca (Guatemala), 29
Mansur, Merwin Belgassen, 72
Marquez, Israel, 31
Martínez, Ana María, 59-60
Mehddawi, Omran Al, 71
Mendizabal, Marlon, 31
Mexico, 21
Mohr, Alberto Fuentes, 29
Monsanto, Carlos Alarcón, 31
Montenegro, President Méndez, 28-29
Montt, President Efraín Riós, 32-33
Mosse, Miguel Angel, 55
*Movimiento de Izquierda
    Revolucionaria* (Chile), 21
Movimiento de Liberación Nacional
    (Guatemala), 28
Muntasser, Abdullatif, 70

Nafi', Mahmoud Abdul Salam, 70, 79
Nahdatul Ulama (Indonesia), 24, 36
Namibia, 20
Nasution, General, 23, 35, 37
Naxalites *see* Communist Party of
    India (Marxist-Leninist)
Nguema, President Masie, 10-11
Nim, Hu, 43
Ningayo, Mayor Karhyom, 20
Nol, Lon, 38
Norren, Dirk van, 100
Nyerere, President, 46

Obote, President Milton, 18, 44, 46,
    47, 48
Oboth-Ofumbi, Charles, 46
ORDEN see *Frente Democrático
    Nacionalista*
Oryema, Lieutenant-Colonel Wilson,
    46
Osorio, President Carlos Arana, 29-30

Paino, Salvador, 52
Partido Socialista de los Trabajadores
    (Argentina), 59
Pena, Rolando Andrade, 30
People's Democratic Party
    (Afghanistan), 15
People's Mujahadeen Organization of
    Iran, 19
Perón, President Juan Domingo, 51
Perón, President María Estela
    Martínez de, 51, 52

perpetrators
    army, 4, 11, 12-13, 15-16, 17-18,
        19-21, 22, 23-24, 27, 35-38, 44,
        49, 50, 52, 55-56, 101, 109-111
    assassins, 18, 69-77
    "death squads", 11, 17-18, 21,
        27-29, 31, 51-52
    opposition groups, 22-23, 24, 28
    paramilitary units and unofficial
        agents, 11-12, 17-18, 21, 24, 36,
        51-52, 103, 110
    police and non-military security
        forces, 11, 12, 17-21, 23-24, 27,
        28, 31, 32-33, 44-49, 61, 64, 101,
        109-111
    prison personnel, 10, 11
Philippines, the, 12, 78
Phim, So, 41
political beliefs and activities, 11, 12,
    13-14, 17-18, 19-21, 23-25, 27-33,
    34-43, 44-49, 50-60, 61-68, 69-77
Pot, Pol, 39, 41, 42
Primatesta, Cardinal, 55
Public Safety Unit (Uganda), 44, 45,
    46
Pucheta, José A., 56

Quevedo, Pedro Quevedo y, 31

Ramadan, Muhammad Mustapha, 70
Rega, José López, 52
religion, 15, 19, 22-23, 24, 41-42, 94
Republic of Korea, 22
Río, Victor González del, 58
Riveros, General Santiago Omar, 53
Rtemi, Salem, 69

Sary, Ieng, 42-43
Sgandurra, Carlos, 56
Shaha, Shambynath, 63
Simbajon, Epifanio, 78
Siedle, Robert, 9
South Africa, 20
South Korea *see* Republic of Korea
South West Africa People's
    Organisation, 20
Ssebunya, Enos, 45
Stoel, Max van der, 100
Stroh, Nicholas, 9
Sudomo, Admiral, 24, 38
Suharto, General, 23, 35, 37
Sukarno, President, 35, 37

For more information on Amnesty International's work, particularly in the US and Canadian sections, or a complete listing of AI's publications with dollar prices, write to:

USA: Amnesty International USA
National Office, Publications Dept.
304 West 58th Street
New York, NY 10019

CANADA: Amnesty International
Canadian Section (English-speaking)
294 Albert Street, Suite 204
Ottawa, Ontario K1P 6E6

Amnistie Internationale
Section canadienne (*francophone*)
1800 Ouest, Boulevard Dorchester
local 400
Montreal, Quebec H3H 2H2